CW01082434

# 111

# SOUP MAKER
# RECIPES

Simple, Healthy, Delicious and Affordable Recipes.
Vegetarian, Low Calorie, Low Carbs, Hot & Cold Soup
Maker Recipes Book for all cooking levels.

2022

# Contents

INTRODUCTION 5
POTATO AND ONION SOUP WITH CHEDDAR CHEESE 9
APPLE AND CELERY SOUP WITH CELERY CHIPS 10
CREAMY CHIVE AND CELERY SOUP 12
PEA PUREE SOUP 13
EASY VEGETABLE SOUP 14
PAN-ASIAN TOFU SOUP 15
COCONUTTY COURGETTE SOUP 17
CARROT AND GINGER SOUP 19
HOMEMADE CREAMY MUSHROOM SOUP 21
HOMEMADE LENTIL SOUP WITH CHILLI OIL 23
EASY SWEETCORN SOUP 25
APPLE-CARROT-GINGER SOUP 27
CREAMY POTATO AND PEAR SOUP 28
PUMPKIN SOUP WITH ALMOND FLAKES 29
HOMEMADE RADISH LEAF SOUP 31
CREAMY CELERY SOUP 32
QUICK ORANGE SOUP 33
LENTIL AND POTATO SOUP WITH BASIL CROUTONS 34
VEGETABLE AND LENTIL STEW WITH PEAS 35
TOMATO SOUP WITH CHICKEN BREAST AND VEGETABLES 36
GREEN ASPARAGUS SOUP WITH PARMESAN AND TRUFFLE FOAM 37
COD AND PUMPKIN SOUP WITH POTATOES 39
VEGAN CREAMY SOUP WITH BROCCOLI 41
THAI SHRIMP GINGER SOUP 43
SPINACH SOUP 44
SUN-DRIED TOMATOES AND BASIL SOUP 45
MOROCCAN VEGETABLE SOUP WITH CHICKPEAS 46
RAMEN NOODLE SOUP 48
GREEN VEGETABLE SOUP WITH YOGHURT 49
CARROT SOUP WITH MANGO 50
CREAMY CARROT SOUP WITH WALNUTS 51
CREAMY PARSNIPS SOUP WITH CROUTONS 52
CAULIFLOWER SOUP WITH RICE AND POTATOES 53
CAULIFLOWER SOUP WITH MACKEREL FILLETS 54
CREAMY ROCKET SOUP WITH PARMESAN 55
COURGETTE SOUP WITH YOGHURT 56
CARROT SOUP WITH ORANGE AND CHILLI 57
TOMATO COCONUT SOUP WITH PRAWNS 58
POTATO MINCE SOUP WITH MUSHROOMS 59
TOMATO AND PEPPER SOUP 60
EASY AND LAZY BEETROOT SOUP 61

SIMPLY DELICIOUS MUSHROOM SOUP 62
SUPER EASY YOGURT SOUP 63
CREAMY RADISH SOUP 64
ONE-POT TOMATO SOUP 65
QUICK BROCCOLI SOUP 66
EASY CHICKEN SOUP 67
EFFORTLESS ASIAN SPICY LENTIL SOUP 68
CURRIED BRUSSELS SPROUTS SOUP 69
MIXED BEANS SOUP WITH SWEET POTATOES 70
TURMERIC STEW 71
VERMICELLI SOUP 72
ITALIAN-STYLE TOMATO SOUP 73
VEGAN CARROT AND PARSNIP CREAMY SOUP 74
LIGHT AND CREAMY SPINACH SOUP 75
SMOOTH AND EASY LEEK AND POTATO SOUPERROR! BOOKMARK NOT DEFINED.
TOMATO SOUP WITH CHIVES 76
ARTICHOKE CREAM SOUP 77
PUMPKIN AND GINGER SOUP 78
CREAMY FENNEL SOUP WITH SCALLOPS 79
ASPARAGUS SOUP 81
WATERCRESS SOUP 82
MISO SOUP 83
PUMPKIN AND GINGER SOUP 84
POTATO SOUP WITH EMMENTHAL CHEESE 85
FAST FISH SOUP WITH VEGETABLES 86
CREAMY CHIVE SOUP 87
SAUERKRAUT SOUP 88
KALE SOUP 89
ONION SOUP 90
IMMUNE BOOSTER SOUP 91
MULLIGATAWNY SOUP 92
CHICKEN AND VEGETABLE SOUP 93
CHRISTMAS BRUSSELS SPROUTS SOUP 94
COUNTRY FARM POTATO SOUP 95
PARSNIP SOUP 96
CREAMY CARROT SOUP WITH NUT CROUTONS 97
BEETROOT SOUP 99
TRADITIONAL CHICKEN SOUP 100
APPLE & CELERY SOUP 101
SPICY CORN SOUP 103
MINESTRONE SOUP 104
MIXED VEGETABLE SOUP 105
BEAN AND CHIVES SOUP 106
POTATO & CARROT SOUP WITH WHITE ASPARAGUS 107
TOFU VEGETABLE POT WITH POTATOES 109

PEA AND HAM SOUP ............................................................ 110
PARSNIP AND APPLE SOUP ................................................ 111
GINGER AND SWEET POTATO SOUP ............................. 112
CREAMY POTATO AND LEEK SOUP ............................... 113
POTATO SOUP WITH MUSHROOMS ............................... 114
CHESTNUT CREAM SOUP ................................................. 115
CABBAGE SOUP .................................................................... 116
WHITE WINE SOUP ............................................................. 117
CREAMY CRESS SOUP ........................................................ 118
CAULIFLOWER, CARROT AND CUMIN SOUP ............... 119
BROCCOLI AND STILTON SOUP ..................................... 120
SUMMER SOUPS .................................................................. 121
COLD CREAMY VEGETABLE SOUP ................................ 122
COLD BEET SOUP WITH EGGS ........................................ 123
TOMATO GAZPACHO WITH CELERY .............................. 124
NO-FUSS STRAWBERRY GAZPACHO ............................. 125
BREAD SOUP WITH DRIED FRUIT AND WHIPPED CREAM ... 126
COLD AVOCADO AND CUCUMBER SOUP ...................... 127
COLD WATERMELON SOUP .............................................. 128
CHILLED TOMATO AND SWEET MELON SOUP ........... 129
CHILLED LEMONY SWEET MELON SOUP .................... 130
COLD CUCUMBER SOUP ................................................... 131
COLD AVOCADO AND CUCUMBER SOUP ...................... 132
ALL ABOUT ERDE: .............................................................. 133
© COPYRIGHT 2022 - ALL RIGHTS RESERVED. ......... 134

Copyrighted Material ©

2022

# Introduction

My journey of traditional soup-making goes a very long way. Well, not as old as the victorian era's cast iron pots and pans on a black leaded fireplace and stones!! But, I would say my interest in cooking started when I was a film student at the university.

I had to be interested in cooking as I hadn't had a choice. Because I was away from the comfort of my parent's home for the first time in my life and was a lodger in a house with some drunk fellows from the university, with whom I am still in touch. But, We had no better ideas than calling for takeaways and trying all the possible things that we could get away with a police warning!! Those days were fun, but I had little money to sustain that lifestyle for a long time. Well, I have never been scavenging in the back alley of a Dominos and fighting over a dried pepperoni pizza type of broke. But still, I had some days to remind me of what the great potato famine was like in a different century...

Many of us go through a journey of self-discovery in different stages of our lives. So I taught myself how to cook... I had to do it purely to be in control of my finances and learn how to fend for myself. I used hobs and pans like everybody else and tried to be more adventurous on payday with the different ingredients.

I am curious by nature; I have always been... I learn a lot by seeing and being in a place that excites me the most. I really love experiencing different cuisines and meeting locals anywhere I go. When in Rome, do as the Romans do... Understanding their food, lifestyle, architecture, and many other aspects of their cultural identities drives me to explore more. I made friends worldwide and shared my passion for food with them. This book results from these travels and good experiences accumulated over the years.

I could have written these recipes in the most traditional way of soup making.
Traditional soup-making way, I meant that you must first saute the ingredients in a saucepan, especially onions and garlic. Then, you

add the ingredients for further sauteing and finish the process by adding the stock later. After 15-30 minutes, the soup is all done.
But at the same time, you had to wait by the hob and stir it constantly so it won't burn and stick to the bottom of the pan.

I am a lazy guy with a hectic lifestyle; I have a full-time job to pay the expenses, and I know that time is money. Time is also the most expensive currency in the universe, with no interest and chance of accrual. So, once it's gone, it's gone; I'd suggest you better make the best of it.

I always find making soup in a traditional sense really time-consuming. But I love food and my soups with a fine slice of toasted bread in the morning, at lunchtime or at dinner. So I had to put up with this traditional cooking process until….

I got one soup maker for myself with the suggestion of a friend.

She told me about soup makers nearly five years ago; until then, I wasn't aware of soup makers at all. She promised me I would love to use a soup maker -this statement usually puts me right off the subject. But I didn't want to say anything to her at that time- My sceptic alarm bells rang, and I wasn't so sure to invest that amount of money that could be a fad. But I knew deep inside that I needed one or at least to try it once.

Saving time from cooking my favourite food? Would this be possible?  How can I stop spending more time by the hob, hopelessly stirring the pots and pans?

While my dinner is cooking in the soup maker, How could I get  20-30  minutes of my life back?
I started to think about what I could do within these 30 minutes. I will not spend one second by the hob, that's for sure.  I can start watching the latest episode of my fav TV show, call my parents, feed the cat, have a shower or snooze. Possibilities are endless…

Soup makers save you a tremendous amount of time from washing up pots and pans.

I love putting all the ingredients in the soup maker and putting my feet up for 30 minutes until my soup is ready, blended, and hot.

It has been nearly five years since I had my soup maker, and I think this is the best investment I have made in the kitchen department. You don't have to splash loads of money on soup makers to do these recipes. I still use my good old, 1.4 lt, very basic but reliable soup maker.

After I fell in love with the practicality of my soup maker, I decided to gather some ideas to create this book and share the recipes with you. So, you can get the best out of your soup maker.

There are still some recipes that you might need to saute for the best of the flavours. However, you can get a soup maker with a "saute" function which is more expensive but helps you to saute the ingredients without using pans and pots.

For most recipes, you don't have to use sauteing; you need to chuck everything into the soup maker and/or follow the recipe preparation instructions.

Soup makers bring so much simplicity and practicality and add value to our daily lives.

This book contains 111 Easy, healthy and super delicious soup recipes designed for soup makers. You will have fantastic tasting soups with the comfort of your soup maker in less than 30 minutes.

**Breakfast**: Great start to a day full of goodness from fresh ingredients. On winter days, they are perfect. It only takes 30 minutes for most recipes. You can always take some with you to work. It will be healthier and cheaper than your daily coffee

**Lunch:** I prefer a light lunch, so I eat it with some salami, olives and cheese board. I pick and mix. They are my favourite mid-day snacks. Try serving your favourite soup with a warm fresh baguette at lunch. Soups go well with nearly everything...

**Dinner**: Soups could be starters for a feast or can be enjoyed on their own as a meal. An affordable, satisfying and slimming close to the day. Who can say no to a healthy soup and a slice of bread prepared in 30 minutes after a hard day at work at school? It is cheaper and faster than a takeaway. Making your own soup is a healthier option than a takeaway because you know what's going into your food.

These soup recipes are incredibly satisfying. They are made with fresh ingredients that are available in your fridge, or use the ingredients in your freezer.

You don't need to worry about complicated cooking processes or time and money-consuming recipes. These recipes are designed for everyone and for all cooking levels. They are so easy to make, and you don't need any experience in cooking... Students, busy professionals, and single working parents who own a soup maker can start cooking instantly and have a bowl of nutritious soup in less than 30 minutes.

Hope you enjoy these recipes. It is my pleasure to share these recipes with my fellow soup junkies.


Erde Herald

# Potato and Onion Soup with Cheddar Cheese

- Cooking time 30 min
- Servings: 4
- Diet: Vegetarian

## *Ingredients:*

- 400 g potatoes
- 2 onions (large)
- 2 clove (s) of garlic
- 2 tablespoons of Ghee/butter or vegetable oil
- 150 g Mature Cheddar/substitutes (Comté, Edam, Emmental)
- 1 l of vegetable stock (2 vegetable cubes dissolved)
- 1 dash of white vinegar
- ½ teaspoon salt
- ¼ teaspoon pepper
- 1 bunch of chives
- 1 bay leaf
- 1 sprig (s) of thyme or pinch of dried thyme

## *Preparation:*

1. Peel and finely chop the onions and garlic.
2. Wash and peel the potatoes and cut them into small cubes.
3. Grate the cheddar cheese and set it aside.
4. Heat some oil in a large pan (if your soup maker has the "Saute" option, use that instead)
5. Add onions and garlic and saute them for 2-3 minutes on medium heat.
6. Add the potatoes, cook them for 5 minutes, and add a dash of vinegar.
7. Slowly stir in the grated cheese and mix with the sauteed potatoes.
8. Add the vegetable stock, bay leaf, thyme salt and pepper

9. Please check the Max and Min lines (see the manufacturing guidelines) and adjust the fluid accordingly. Don't exceed the maximum limit or below. It's best to keep it between the minimum and maximum levels.
10. Choose the "Smooth" setting.
11. Open the lid and add grated cheese to your hot soup.
12. Choose the "Blend" setting and blend it until it is creamy. Finely chop the chives and garnish the soup with more cheddar cheese.

# Apple and Celery Soup with Celeriac Chips

- Cooking time: 25- 30 min
- Serves: 4
- Diet: Vegetarian

## *Ingredients:*

### *For the soup:*

- 500 g celery
- 1 apple
- 1 potato
- 100 ml apple juice
- 200 ml single cream
- 500 ml vegetable stock(or water)
- 2 vegetable cubes
- 1/4 teaspoon salt

### *For the chips:*

- 100 g celeriac
- 250 ml of olive oil

## *Preparation:*

1. Put everything into your soup maker except single cream.
2. Please check the Max and Min lines (see the manufacturing guidelines) and adjust the fluid accordingly. Don't exceed the maximum limit or below. It's best to keep it between the minimum and maximum levels.
3. Set your soup maker to a "Smooth" setting.
4. While your soup is cooking in the soup maker, start cooking the celeriac chips.
5. Cut the celery into thin slices, fry them in hot fat to make chips, and drain briefly on kitchen paper (Use an Air fryer for a lighter option)
6. Once the soup is cooked, add single cream to your soup and stir it well.
7. Taste and season to taste.
8. Serve apple and celery soup with celeriac chips.

# Creamy Chives and Celery Soup

- Cooking time: 30 min
- Servings: 2-4
- Diet: Vegetarian

## *Ingredients:*

- 350 g onions chopped
- 250 g celeriac chopped
- 1 tablespoon vegetable oil
- 1 l vegetable stock
- 300 ml single cream
- Salt
- Pepper
- 1 bunch of chives

## *Preparation:*

1. Peel the onion and cut it into 1 cm cubes.
2. Wash, peel and clean celeriac and cut into 1 cm pieces.
3. Put vegetable oil in a pan and add chopped onions. Saute the onion for two minutes on medium heat. (if your soup maker has the "Saute" option, use that instead)
4. Add finely chopped celeriac and cook for further 4 minutes.
5. Decant the onions and celeriac cubes from the pan to your soup maker.
6. Add vegetable stock and choose the "Smooth" setting.
7. Once cooked, add 300 ml single cream and stir it well.
8. Season with salt and pepper.
9. Wash the chives, shake dry and cut into fine rolls.
10. Serve with a sprinkle of chives.

# Pea Puree Soup

- Cooking Time: 25-30 minutes
- Serves: 2- 4
- Diet: Vegetarian

## *Ingredients:*

- 1 medium-size potato (cut into small cubes)
- 1 medium-size pc. carrots (peeled and chopped)
- 400 g. green peas (Frozen or Fresh )
- 1 l vegetable stock
- 3 tablespoons flour (mix with 100 ml water)
- 1 tablespoon- Ghee or butter
- Salt and pepper (for seasoning)
- Parsley – 1 bunch chopped(for garnishing)

## *Preparation:*

1. Put everything into your soup maker except parsley(for garnishing).
2. Please check the Max and Min lines and adjust the fluid accordingly. Don't exceed the maximum limit; keep the fluid between the minimum and maximum levels.
3. Set your soup maker to a "Smooth" setting.
4. Once cooked, add soft cheese to your soup and blend it for 10 seconds.
5. Taste and season to taste.
6. Serve it with some chopped parsley.

# Easy Vegetable Soup

- Cooking time: 20 min
- Serves: 2-4
- Diet: Vegetarian

## *Ingredients:*

- 1 can of (drained 200-250 g) white beans
- 350 g of frozen mixed vegetables (Carrots, Garden Peas, Sweetcorn etc.)
- 1 small onion chopped
- 1 tablespoon vegetable oil
- 750-litre water
- 2 vegetable broth cubes
- 1 bay leaf (optional)
- 1/8 teaspoon white pepper
- ½ teaspoon salt
- 200g light herb soft processed cheese of your choice
- Salt and extra pepper (for seasoning)

## *Preparation:*

1. Put everything into your soup maker except soft cheese. (You may want to saute the onion with 1 tablespoon of vegetable oil, but it is totally up to you)
2. Please check the Max and Min lines and adjust the fluid accordingly. Don't exceed the maximum limit; keep the fluid between the minimum and maximum levels.
3. Set your soup maker to a "Smooth" setting.
4. Once cooked, add soft cheese to your soup and blend it for 10 seconds intervals.
5. Taste and season to taste.

# Pan-Asian Tofu Soup

- Cooking time 15 to 30 min
- Servings:2- 4
- Diet: Vegetarian, Vegan, Low Calorie

## *Ingredients:*

- 200 g tofu
- 2 carrots
- 1 stick (s) leek (small)
- 100 g pea pods
- 150 g mushrooms
- 750 ml water
- ½ inch ginger
- ¼ teaspoon salt
- ¼ teaspoon white pepper
- 2 tablespoons light soy sauce
- 1 teaspoon peanut oil
- 1 teaspoon sesame oil

## *Preparation:*

1. Clean, wash and flake the carrots.
2. Then clean, wash and quarter the mushrooms.
3. Finally, slice the leek, peel and finely chop the ginger.
4. Cut the tofu into 1 cm cubes.
5. Heat the oil in a saucepan.
6. Sauté the vegetables and tofu for 3 minutes in a pan.
7. Pour everything into your soup maker and add water.
8. Please check the Max and Min lines and adjust the fluid accordingly. Don't exceed the maximum limit or below the minimum. Changing the fluid level to keep it between the minimum and maximum levels is best.
9. Choose the "Chunky" mode.

10. Once cooked, season the Asian tofu soup with salt and pepper. Then, drizzle over more sesame oil and soy sauce to taste.

# Coconutty Courgette Soup

- Cooking time 15 to 30 min
- Servings: 4
- Diet: Vegetarian

## *Ingredients:*

- 600 g courgette(aka zucchini)
- 1 small onion -chopped
- 2 tablespoon coconut oil
- 800-litre vegetable broth
- 1 can (s) of coconut milk (approx. 400 ml)
- 200-gram soft cheese
- 1 stick (s) lemongrass
- ¼ teaspoon salt
- ¼ teaspoon white pepper

## *Preparation:*

1. Wash the courgettes, and cut them into small cubes.
2. Bash the woody bottom part of the fresh lemongrass with a pestle. Keep it intact, just enough to let infuse the flavour into the soup.
3. Heat the coconut oil in a pan on medium heat. (If your soup maker has a "saute" setting, use that option)
4. Add lemongrass and stir fry for a minute. This process will help lemongrass to release its fragrance.
5. Add chopped onions and cook them for 2 minutes.
6. Add courgettes to the pan and cook for further 3 minutes.
7. Transfer this mixture to your soup maker.
8. Pour vegetable broth and coconut milk into your soup maker.
9. Please check the Max and Min lines and adjust the fluid accordingly.

10. Don't exceed the maximum limit or below the minimum. It's best to adjust the fluid level to keep it between the minimum and maximum levels. Choose the "Chunky" setting on your soup maker.
11. Once cooked, open the lid and carefully remove the lemongrass with a tong. Be careful as it will be hot.
12. Add soft cheese, salt and pepper.
13. Season to taste and serve.

# Carrot and Ginger soup

- Cooking time 15 to 30 min
- Servings: 4
- Diet: Vegetarian

## *Ingredients:*

- 1 medium-size onion
- 2 cloves of garlic
- 2 tablespoons olive oil
- 600 g carrots
- 1 l of vegetable stock
- ½ teaspoon of salt
- ¼ teaspoon of black pepper
- 1-inch ginger (fresh, small)
- 2 tablespoons Crème Fraiche (or 1 dash of whipped cream)
- 1 orange (juice)

## *Preparation:*

1. Peel the onion, garlic and carrots and cut them into small cubes.
2. Peel the ginger and grate it finely or cut it into small cubes.
3. Heat some olive oil in a pan and sauté the onions together with the garlic until translucent.
4. Add the ginger and carrots and cook further 3 minutes.
5. Season with salt and pepper.
6. Transfer it to your soup maker (If you have the "Saute" option, use that option)
7. Please check the Max and Min lines and adjust the fluid accordingly. Don't exceed the maximum limit or below the minimum. Changing the fluid level to keep it between the minimum and maximum levels is best.
8. Choose " Smooth" mode
9. Once cooked, open the lid and add the juice of the squeezed orange.
10. Choose "Blend" mode and blend the soup until it is creamy and smooth.

11. Season the soup to taste with a bit of Crème Fraiche and serve hot.

# Homemade Creamy Mushroom Soup

- Cooking time: 25 min
- Servings: 2-4
- Diet: Vegetarian, Vegan

## *Ingredients:*

- 400 gr mushrooms (fresh, frozen, or 2 X drained cans)
- 150 ml single cream /150 ml soy cream for vegan option
- 2 tablespoons of vegetable oil
- 1 medium-size onion chopped
- 2 tablespoons of flour( 100 ml of cold water to make a paste)
- 1 l water or  mushroom stock (2 mushroom cubes dissolved in 1 l water)
- 2-3 cloves of garlic
- 1 teaspoon salt
- 1 teaspoon of black pepper
- 1 teaspoon of thyme
- 1 pinch of chilli powder

### Preparation:

1. Slice (if you are using fresh). 400 g of mushrooms.
2. Chop garlic and onions into small sizes.
3. Put 2 tablespoons of olive oil in a large saucepan and saute the onions and garlic for two minutes (If you have a "Sauté" option, please use that option)
4. Add mushrooms to the pan and cook further 5 minutes on medium heat.
5. Decant the ingredients in the pan to your soup maker.
6. Dissolve flour into 100ml of cold water. This is a thickening agent, and it will make your soup thicker. Add salt, black pepper, thyme, chilli powder and flour paste to your soup
7. Add 1 litre of water (or mushroom stock) and close the lid.
8. Please check the Max and Min lines and adjust the fluid accordingly. Don't exceed the maximum limit or below the

minimum. It's best to accommodate the fluid level to keep it between the minimum and maximum levels.

9. Choose "Smooth" mode.
10. Once cooked, open the lid and add 150ml cream into your soup and stir it well.

# Homemade Lentil Soup with Chilli Oil

- Cooking time: 30 min
- Servings: 2-4
- Diet: Vegetarian, Vegan

## *Ingredients:*

- 340 g red lentils
- 1 l water or vegetable stock
- 1 medium onion
- 1 carrot
- 1 potato (medium size)
- 2 tablespoons of tomato paste
- 1 teaspoon of salt
- 1 teaspoon of black pepper
- 2 tablespoons of vegetable oil
- 1 ½ tablespoon of chilli flakes
- ½ lemon juice (optional)

## *Preparation:*

1. Wash red lentils very well and put them into your soup maker.
2. Peel and chop the carrot, onion and potato in small sizes and add them to your soup maker.
3. Add tomato paste, salt and black pepper.
4. Cover it with water or vegetable stock.
5. Please check the Max and Min lines and adjust the fluid accordingly. Don't exceed the maximum limit or below the minimum. It's best to accommodate the fluid level to keep it between these levels.
6. Close the lid and choose the "Smooth" setting.
7. Once cooked, check the consistency of the lentil soup; if it is too thick, add some more water.
8. Heat the butter in a pan and add the chilli flakes into the pan while it is bubbling. Stir for 10 seconds and turn off the heat.
9. Serve your lentil soup in a bowl and drizzle the chilli oil.

10. Squeeze half a lemon juice over the soup. Lemon juice always brings the best of lentils.

# Easy Sweetcorn Soup

- Cooking time: 30 minutes
- Serving: 4-6
- Diet: Vegetarian

## *Ingredients:*

- 600 gr frozen or fresh corn
- 4-6 medium size potatoes (cut into small sizes)
- 1 large onion
- 2 tablespoons of corn oil or rapeseed oil
- 1 l water or vegetable stock
- 4 tablespoons of light cream cheese
- 1 teaspoon salt
- ½ teaspoon white pepper
- 2 limes or 1 lemon juice
- Fresh Parsley or Coriander (to garnish)

## *Preparation:*

1. Cut the onion and potatoes into small pieces
2. Heat 2 tablespoons of corn or rapeseed oil into the pan and add onions.
3. Fry onions until they are soft on a medium heat
4. Add the potatoes and fry them for further 3 minutes.
5. Add the frozen corn to the pan (if you are using fresh corn from a can, skip this step), and stir fry with other ingredients for 5 minutes.
6. Transfer the mixture to your soup maker.
7. Add water or vegetable stock, salt, and white pepper.
8. Please check the Max and Min lines and adjust the fluid accordingly. Don't exceed the maximum limit or below the minimum. It's best to accommodate the fluid level to keep it between these levels.
9. Set to "Smooth" mode.
10. Once cooked, check If the soup is blended well.
11. Add light soft cream cheese and stir it well.

12. Season to taste.
13. Garnish with herbs of your choice and squeeze some lime juice over it.

# Apple-Carrot-Ginger Soup

- Cooking time 15 to 30 min
- Servings: 2-4
- Diet: Vegeterian, Vegan

## Ingredients:

- 1 onion (large)
- 2 clove (s) of garlic
- 500 g carrots
- 1 ½ inch ginger (finely) chopped
- 1 lemon (juice)
- 2 apples
- 250 ml white wine (dry Pinot Grigio, Pinot Gris, Sauvignon Blanc,)
- 1 l vegetable stock
- 1 tablespoon vegetable oil
- ½ teaspoon salt
- ¼ teaspoon white pepper

## Preparation:

1. Peel the onion, garlic, carrots, ginger and apples and cut them into small pieces. Drizzle the peeled apples with lemon juice. Stir the mixture well and set it aside.
2. Fry onion and garlic in 1 tablespoon of oil in a pan until they are translucent (if your soup maker has the "Sauté" option, use that instead)
3. Transfer them into your soup maker
4. Add carrots, ginger and apples into the onion and garlic mixture.
5. Pour wine and vegetable stock.
6. Please check the Max and Min lines and adjust the fluid accordingly. Don't exceed the maximum limit or below the minimum. It's best to accommodate the fluid level to keep it between these levels.
7. Set to "Smooth" mode.
8. Once cooked, check the soup if it is blended very well.
9. Season to taste.

# Creamy Potato and Pear Soup

- Cooking time 15 to 30 min
- Servings: 4-6
- Diet: Vegetarian, Vegan

## *Ingredients:*

- 500 g potatoes
- 500 g pears
- 1 onion
- 200 ml single cream /Vegan: Soy cream
- 1 tablespoon of vegetable oil
- 1 l of vegetable broth
- ½ teaspoon salt.
- ½ teaspoon pepper.

## *Preparation:*

1. Peel the potatoes, onions and pears. Then, core the pears and cut everything into small cubes.
2. Sauté the onion in 1 tablespoon of vegetable oil in a pan (if your soup maker has the "Sauté" option, use that instead)
3. Transfer it to your soup maker
4. Add all the ingredients except cream
5. Choose "Smooth" mode
6. Once cooked, add the single cream/soy cream and stir it well.
7. Season to taste and serve.

# Pumpkin Soup with Almond Flakes

- Cooking time 15 to 30 min
- Servings: 4
- Diet: Vegetarian, Vegan

## *Ingredients:*

- 600 g pumpkin (cut into small sizes)
- 1 onion
- 1 tablespoon of vegetable oil
- 1 l of vegetable stock
- 250 ml single cream / Vegan: Soy cream
- 2-3 drops of almond extract
- 3 tablespoon almond flakes
- Salt and pepper to taste

## *Preparation:*

1. Peel the pumpkin and onion, and chop them into small sizes.
2. Sauté in a saucepan with oil until the onion is translucent. (If your soup maker has a "Sauté" option, use that option instead)
3. Transfer it to your soup maker.
4. Add all the ingredients except cream.
5. Please check the Max and Min lines and adjust the fluid accordingly. Don't exceed the maximum limit or below the minimum. It's best to accommodate the fluid level to keep it between these levels.
6. Choose "Smooth" mode
7. Once cooked, add cream and stir it well.
8. Pour almond flakes into a hot pan, and constantly stir until they are light brown.
9. Serve your soup with a sprinkle of roasted almond flakes.

**If you are enjoying this product, please leave us a review on Amazon:**

**How to leave us a review?**
1- Go to your Amazon Account
2- Click "Your Orders"
3- Find and click this product
4- Click on "Write a product review."

**Your opinion matters to us!!!**
We are happy to take your words on board and listen to your ideas. This is so important for us to develop more product ideas according to your needs in the future.

If you enjoy this product and/or have any suggestions. Please contact us at contact@evepublishing.co.uk

# Homemade Radish Leaf Soup

- Cooking time 15 to 30 min
- Servings: 4
- Diet: Vegetarian

## *Ingredients:*

- 3 bunch of radishes (with leaves)
- 1 medium onion
- 1 large potato
- 50 g butter
- 1 tablespoon flour
- 1 l of water
- 2 vegetable cubes
- 200 ml single cream
- ½ teaspoon salt
- ½ teaspoon black pepper
- A pinch of nutmeg

## *Preparation:*

1. Wash the radishes, remove the leaves and chop. Roughly chop the radishes.
2. Finely dice the onion and potato.
3. Melt the butter, add the radishes, potato and onion and sauté without taking any colour. (If your soup maker has a "Sauté" option, use that option instead)
4. Scatter the flour and sauté briefly.
5. Transfer the ingredients into your soup maker.
6. Pour the water and vegetable cubes and season with salt, pepper and nutmeg.
7. Please check the Max and Min lines and adjust the fluid accordingly. Don't exceed the maximum limit or below the minimum. It's best to adjust the fluid level to keep it between these levels.

- Choose "Smooth" mode
- Once cooked, add the single cream and stir it well.
- Season to taste.

# Creamy Celery Soup

- Cooking time: 30 minutes
- Servings: 2-4
- Diet: Vegetarian, Vegan

## *Ingredients:*

- 400 g celery - chopped
- 1 large potato- chopped
- 1 l of water
- 2 vegetable cubes
- 150 ml single cream/ Vegan: Soy cream
- ¼ teaspoon Nutmeg (grated)
- salt
- pepper

## *Preparation:*

1. For the celery cream soup, wash and peel the celery and potatoes and cut them into small sizes. If your vegetables are smaller in size. Then, they will cook faster in your soup maker.
2. Put your chopped celery and potato in your soup maker.
3. Add water and vegetable cubes.
4. Please check the Max and Min lines and adjust the fluid accordingly.
5. Don't exceed the maximum limit; keep the fluid between the minimum and maximum levels.
6. Cook it under the "Smooth" setting.
7. Once cooked, make sure the soup is very smooth.
8. Add the cream and nutmeg and stir it well.
9. Season to taste before serving.

# Quick Orange Soup

- Cooking time: 30min
- Servings: 2-4
- Diet: Vegetarian, Low Calorie

## *Ingredients:*

- 400 g Cauliflower
- 2 large Oranges
- 150 cottage cheese (fat-free for low-calorie option)
- 150 g carrots
- 100 g Mozzarella cheese(reduced fat for low-calorie alternative)
- 25 gr fresh ginger chopped
- 1 l water or vegetable broth
- ½ teaspoon salt
- ¼ teaspoon black pepper

## *Preparation:*

1. Chop cauliflower heads into bite-size.
2. Grate coarsely carrots, ginger and chop mozzarella cheese
3. Finely grate the orange zest, squeeze the juice, and chop the orange peel.
4. Add everything to your soup maker.
5. Please check the Max and Min lines and adjust the fluid accordingly.
6. Don't exceed the maximum limit; keep the fluid between the minimum and maximum levels.
7. Choose "Smooth" Setting
8. Check the consistency and blend another 30-45 seconds if necessary
9. Season to taste.

# Lentil and Potato Soup with Basil Croutons

- Cooking Time: 25 min
- Serves: 2-4
- Diet: Vegetarian, Vegan

## *Ingredients:*

**For the soup:**

- 3 carrots
- 250 g potatoes
- 2 tbsp olive oil
- 150 g Red lentils
- ½ tsp turmeric powder
- 1 l vegetable broth
- 60 g tomato paste (4 tbsp)
- Salt & black pepper to taste
- 120 ml single cream (Vegan alternative: Soy cream)

**For the garnish (optional):**

- 5 g basil (chopped- 1 handful)
- 1 tablespoon of vegetable oil
- 1 slice of sourdough bread

## *Preparation:*

**For the soup:**

1. Chop the vegetables and put all the ingredients for the soup into your soup maker.
2. Choose the "Smooth" setting and cook.
3. Once cooked, choose the "Blend" option.
4. Season to taste with salt and pepper.

**For the garnish:**

1. Dice the slices of bread—heat one tablespoon of vegetable oil in the pan. Roast the bread cubes on medium heat for 5 minutes until golden. Wash the basil, shake to dry and pluck the leaves. Fry them with the bread for 2-3 minutes.
2. Pour the soup into a bowl, and sprinkle with bread cubes and basil.

# Vegetable and Lentil Stew with Peas

- Cooking time: 25 min
- Serves: 2
- Diet: Vegetarian, Vegan

## *Ingredients:*

- 5 g ginger (thin sliced)
- 1 shallot (chopped)
- 1 sweet potato- cut into small sizes
- 100 g celery (chopped)
- 100 g red lentils (washed)
- 1 tsp harissa paste
- 1 tbsp tomato paste
- ½ tsp curry powder
- 750 ml vegetable broth
- Salt & pepper to taste
- 1 tbsp coconut milk

**For topping:**
- 2 pieces of spring onions
- 150 g frozen peas
- 2 tsp sunflower seeds

## *Preparation:*

1. Put everything into your soup maker except the ingredients for the topping. (You may saute the onion with one tablespoon of vegetable oil for three minutes, but it is totally up to you).
2. Please check the Max and Min lines and adjust the fluid accordingly. Don't exceed the maximum limit; keep the fluid between the minimum and maximum levels.
3. Set your soup maker to a "Chunky" setting.
4. Once cooked, season to taste.

**For topping:**
1. Clean, wash and chop the spring onions.
2. Heat the one tablespoon of oil in a pan, and fry the spring onion, peas and sunflower seeds for 5 minutes.
3. Fill the soup into two bowls, drizzle with some coconut milk and top with the peas.

# Tomato Soup with Chicken Breasts and Vegetables

- Cooking time: 30 minutes
- Serves: 2-4

## *Ingredients:*

- 400 g tomatoes ( freshly chopped or from a can)
- 1 l chicken broth (or water with 2 chicken cubes dissolved)
- 2 medium carrots (chopped)
- 2 medium potatoes(diced)
- 2 bell peppers (chopped)
- 200 g chickpeas (can; drained weight)
- 4 spring onions (chopped)
- 200-250 g chicken breast fillets (ready to eat, cooked, diced)
- ¼ teaspoon salt
- ¼ teaspoon black pepper
- ½ lemon (juice)
- 1 tsp honey
- 10 g parsley (0.5 bunch) to garnish

## *Preparation:*

1. Put all the ingredients: except parsley, honey and lemon juice.
2. Please check the Max and Min lines  (see the manufacturing guidelines) and adjust the fluid accordingly. Don't exceed the maximum limit or below. Changing the fluid level to keep it between the minimum and maximum levels is best.
3. Choose the "Chunky" setting.
4. Once cooked, squeeze the lemon and add about two tablespoons of juice to the soup along with honey.
5. Finally, wash the parsley, shake dry, finely chop and sprinkle with the soup before serving.

# Green Asparagus Soup with Parmesan and Truffle Foam

- Cooking Time: 30 min
- Serves: 2-4
- Diet: Vegetarian

## *Ingredients:*

- 500 g green asparagus
- 2 shallot or 1 medium onion
- 20 g butter (2 tbsp)
- 750 ml classic vegetable broth
- 60 g parmesan (1 piece)
- 1 lemon
- 100 ml single cream
- ¼ teaspoon salt
- ¼ teaspoon pepper
  **Optional:**
- 100 ml milk (1.5% fat)
- 3 drops of truffle oil

## *Preparation:*

1. Wash and drain the asparagus and cut off any woody ends. Peel the asparagus in the lower third. Cut the sticks into pieces about 2 cm long. Peel and finely chop shallot.
2. Use the "Saute" option or fry the asparagus with chopped shallot in a pan for five minutes over medium heat with one tablespoon of vegetable oil.
3. Put all the ingredients: except single cream, parmesan, milk and truffle oil, into your soup maker.
4. Please check the Max and Min lines (see the manufacturing guidelines) and adjust the fluid accordingly. Don't exceed the maximum limit or below. Changing the fluid level to keep it between the minimum and maximum levels is best.
5. Choose the "Smooth" setting and cook.

6.  Once cooked, add 100 ml cream and stir it well.
7.  Pour into the bowls,  grate some parmesan on top and serve immediately.

**Optional:**

1. Heat the milk, a pinch of salt and truffle oil (to approx. 60 ° C), do not let it boil! Instead, whip the milk until frothy, e.g., with a hand blender, small whisk or electric milk frother. (use long-life milk for the best result).
2. Pour the soup into bowls and distribute the milk foam on top.

# Cod and Pumpkin Soup with Potatoes

- Cooking time: 30 min
- Serves: 2-4

## *Ingredients:*

- 300 g pumpkin
- 400 g waxy potatoes
- 1 leek
- 1 fennel bulb or (1 large thin sliced white onion)
- 2 cloves of garlic
- 2 tbsp olive oil
- 1 tsp mustard seeds
- 1 l vegetable broth
- 400 g cod fillet (you can use pre-cooked cod)
- ½ teaspoon salt
- 1 organic lemon
- ½ teaspoon pepper
- 1 pinch of ground cloves

## *Preparation:*

1. Cut the pumpkin into cubes about 2 cm.
2. Wash and peel the potatoes and cut them into cubes about 2 cm in size.
3. Halve the leek lengthways, wash, clean and cut across into 1 cm wide rings.
4. Wash and clean the fennel and put the greens aside. Halve and quarter the fennel and cut across into fine strips.
5. Peel the garlic and cut it into thin slices.
6. Heat oil in a pot. Add the pumpkin, potatoes, garlic, and mustard seeds, sauté briefly over medium heat. If your soup maker has a "Saute" option, use that instead.
7. Put all the ingredients except lemon and fennel greens.
8. Please check the Max and Min lines (see the manufacturing guidelines) and adjust the fluid accordingly. Don't exceed the maximum limit or below.

Changing the fluid level to keep it between the minimum and maximum levels is best.

9. Choose the "Chunky" setting and cook.
10. Wash the lemon with hot water, rub dry, and grate half of the peel finely. Halve the lemon and squeeze half (use the rest of the lemon otherwise). Pluck the fennel green into small twigs.
11. Season to taste, and add a little lemon juice.
12. Sprinkle with fennel greens and lemon zest, and serve.

# Creamy Vegan Broccoli Soup

- Cooking time: 30 min
- Serves: 2-4
- Diet: Vegan, Vegeterian

## *Ingredients:*

- 1 tbsp coconut oil or olive oil.
- 1 medium onion, chopped
- 2 cloves of garlic
- ¼ tsp chilli pepper flakes
- 900 ml cups vegetable stock
- 1 head of broccoli, stems peeled and chopped, large buds chopped
- 300 g cups spinach leaves or 100g frozen (or 1/2 head of cauliflower, chopped
- 300 ml soy cream
- Lemon juice to taste (about ½ lemon)
- Salt and Pepper to taste

## *Preparation:*

1- Put all the ingredients into your soup maker.
2- Please check the Max and Min lines (see the manufacturing guidelines) and adjust the fluid accordingly. Don't exceed the maximum limit or below. Changing the fluid level to keep it between the minimum and maximum levels is the best.
3- Choose the "Smooth" setting and cook.
4- Season to taste and add lemon juice.
5- Serve with avocado slices (optional) and a warm baguette

## If you are enjoying this product, please leave us a review on Amazon:

### How to leave us a review?
1- Go to your Amazon Account
2- Click "Your Orders"
3- Find and click this product
4- Click on "Write a product review."

### Your opinion matters to us!!!
We are happy to take your words on board and listen to your ideas. This is so important for us to develop more product ideas according to your needs in the future.

If you enjoy this product and/or have any suggestions. Please contact us at contact@evepublishing.co.uk

---

# Thai Shrimp Ginger Soup

- Cooking time: 30 min
- Serves: 2-4

## *Ingredients:*

- 1 tablespoon full of granulated sugar (white sugar)
- 500 g of cooked Shrimp
- 20 g of ginger (thin sliced)
- 1 Birds eye chilli (chopped, deseeded if you prefer less heat)
- 1 stalk lemongrass (bruise the stem with the pestle)
- 1 l chicken stock
- 2 kaffir lime leaves (substitute one lime peeled)
- 1 can coconut milk (400 ml)
- 1 tablespoon of fish sauce (nam pla)
- Limes and coriander (cilantro) (chopped)

## *Preparation:*

1- Put all the ingredients into your soup maker except limes and coriander.
2- Please check the Max and Min lines (see the manufacturing guidelines) and adjust the fluid accordingly. Don't exceed the maximum limit or below. Changing the fluid level to keep it between the minimum and maximum levels is best.
3- Choose the "Chunky" setting and cook.
4- Once cooked, take out the lemongrass with a tong.
5- Cut a lime in half, sprinkle the soup with the chopped coriander(cilantro) and serve with a cut lime.

# Spinach Soup

- Cooking time: 15-20 min
- Serves: 2-4
- Diet: Vegetarian, Vegan

## *Ingredients:*

- 800 g of frozen spinach leaves
- 4 medium-sized potatoes (Cut into small cubes)
- 1 litre of vegetable broth
- 200 ml single cream (Soy cream for Vegan alternative)
- Salt and Pepper to taste

## *Preparation:*

1. Put all the ingredients except cream into your soup maker.
2. Please check your soup maker's max and min lines (see the manufacturing guidelines) and adjust the fluid accordingly. Don't exceed the maximum limit or below. Changing the fluid level to keep it between the minimum and maximum levels is best.
3. Choose the "Smooth" setting and cook
4. Once cooked, add 200 ml of single cream and stir it well.
5. Season to taste and serve hot.

# Sun-Dried Tomatoes and Basil Soup

- Cooking time: 15-20 min
- Serves: 2-4
- Diet: Vegetarian, Vegan

## *Ingredients:*

- 5 ripe tomatoes round (Cut into small size)
- 2 medium onions (cut into small sizes)
- 3 garlic cloves (sliced)
- 8-10 basil leaves
- 225 g Sun-dried tomatoes (marinated in oil- drained)
- 900 ml vegetable stock
- ½ teaspoon sugar
- salt and black pepper to taste.
- ¼ teaspoon paprika,
- 2 tablespoon olive oil

## *Preparation:*

1. Use the Saute option on the soup maker or a saucepan to heat the two tablespoons of olive oil.
2. Saute onion, garlic and tomatoes for 4-5 minutes
3. Transfer the mixture to your soup maker and add the rest of the ingredients.
4. Please check the Max and Min lines (see the manufacturing guidelines) and adjust the fluid accordingly. Don't exceed the maximum limit or below. Changing the fluid level to keep it between the minimum and maximum levels is best.
5. Choose the "Smooth" setting and cook.
6. Once cooked and choose the "Blend" option.
7. Blend for a further 30-45 sec until it is smooth.

# Moroccan Vegetable Soup with Chickpeas

- Cooking time: 15-20 min
- Serves: 2-4
- Diet: Vegetarian, Vegan

## *Ingredients:*

- 1 small onion (diced)
- 3 garlic cloves(sliced)
- 3 sticks of celery (chopped)
- 2 red chilli peppers (chopped)
- 2 tbsp olive oil
- 3 tbsp tomato paste
- 2 tsp ground coriander
- 1 tsp turmeric powder
- ½ tsp cinnamon
- 500 ml water
- 1 vegetable stock cube
- 1 tbsp harissa paste
- 200 g potatoes (1 large potato- diced)
- Salt and black pepper to taste
- 400 g chickpeas (can; drained weight)
- 50 g baby spinach (fresh -frozen)
- 1 handful parsley
- 1 lemon (zest and juice)

## *Preparation:*

1. Put everything into your soup maker except parsley and lemon. (You may want to sauté the onion garlic with one tablespoon of vegetable oil if you have the sauté option on your soup maker. Sautéing process gives extra flavour to the soup.
2. Please check the Max and Min lines and adjust the fluid accordingly. Don't exceed the maximum limit; keep the fluid between the minimum and maximum levels.
3. Set your soup maker to a "Chunky" setting and cook.

4.  Wash the parsley, shake dry and finely chop the leaves. Add parsley to the soup and season with zest, lemon juice, salt, and pepper.
5.  Put the soup in bowls and serve with warm naan bread.

# Ramen Noodles Soup

- Cooking time: 15-20 min
- Serves: 2-4
- Diet: Vegetarian, Vegan

## *Ingredients:*

- 450 g chicken breast fillet (sliced -cooked)
- 4 tbsp sesame oil
- 30 ml of rice wine (Sake)
- 3 tbsp soy sauce
- 1 tbsp mirin (sweet rice wine)
- 200 g ramen noodles
- A pinch of salt
- 2 eggs (hard-boiled)
- 1 chilli pepper (sliced)
- 1 spring onion (sliced)
- 250 g a can of mushrooms (drained, e.g. oyster mushrooms,)
- 2 garlic cloves (thinly sliced)
- 20 g ginger (thinly sliced)
- 800 ml of poultry broth
- ¼ teaspoon pepper
- 1 tbsp toasted sesame seeds (15 g)

## *Preparation:*

1. Put everything into your soup maker except eggs and sesame seeds.
2. Please check the Max and Min lines and adjust the fluid accordingly. Don't exceed the maximum limit; keep the fluid between the minimum and maximum levels.
3. Set your soup maker to a "Chunky" setting.
4. Once cooked, taste and season it with salt and pepper.
5. Serve with halved eggs and sprinkle sesame seeds on top.

# Green Vegetable Soup with Yoghurt

- Cooking time: 15-20 min
- Serves: 2-4
- Diet: Vegetarian

## *Ingredients:*

- 600 g frozen peas
- 4 stems of mint (chopped- save some to garnish)
- 1 l water
- 2 vegetable cubes
- 200 g greek yoghurt
- 120 g mushrooms (canned-drained)
- 3 tbsp olive oil
- 100 g sugar snap
- Salt and Pepper to taste

## *Preparation:*

1. Put everything into your soup maker except greek yoghurt.
2. Please check the Max and Min lines and adjust the fluid accordingly. Don't exceed the maximum limit; keep the fluid between the minimum and maximum levels.
3. Set your soup maker to a "Smooth" setting.
4. Once cooked, add yoghurt and blend it for 10 seconds until it is smooth.
5. Taste and season it with salt and pepper.
6. Serve with some mint leaves on top with warm sourdough bread.

# Carrot Soup with Mango

- Cooking time: 15-20 min
- Serves: 2-4
- Diet: Vegetarian, Vegan

## *Ingredients:*

- 30 g ginger (1 piece- thinly chopped)
- 400 g carrots (4 carrots) (peeled, thinly chopped)
- 1 tbsp olive oil
- 1 mango (sliced)
- A can of coconut milk (400 ml)
- 250 ml water
- ½ teaspoons salt
- A pinch of white pepper
- 1 spring onion (sliced- for garnishing)

## *Preparation:*

1. Put everything into your soup maker except spring onions.
2. Please check the Max and Min lines and adjust the fluid accordingly. Don't exceed the maximum limit; keep the fluid between the minimum and maximum levels.
3. Set your soup maker to a "Smooth" setting.
4. Once cooked, add soft cheese to your soup and blend it for 10 seconds intervals.
5. Season to taste.
6. Clean, wash and cut the spring onions into fine rings and add a little pepper as you like.
7. Serve hot with spring onion as garnishing

# Creamy Carrot Soup with Walnuts

- Cooking time: 15-20 min
- Serves: 2-4
- Diet: Vegetarian, Vegan

## Ingredients:

- 200 g beetroot (pre-cooked, vacuumed)
- 1 red onion
- 500 g carrots (or parsnips)
- 1 tbsp rapeseed oil
- 650 ml water
- 2 vegetable cubes
- 45 g walnut kernels (3 tbsp)
- 4 branches of thyme (for garnishing)
- Salt & black pepper to taste
- A pinch of nutmeg
- 100 ml sour cream (Soy cream for Vegan option)

## Preparation:

1. Put everything into your soup maker except thyme and cream.
2. Please check the Max and Min lines and adjust the fluid accordingly. Don't exceed the maximum limit; keep the fluid between the minimum and maximum levels.
3. Set your soup maker to a "Smooth" setting.
4. Once cooked, add cream and stir well.
5. Season to taste.
6. Serve with some thyme branches on top.

# Creamy Parsnips Soup with Croutons

- Cooking time: 30 min
- Serves: 2-4
- Diet: Vegetarian

## *Ingredients:*

- 400 g parsnips (diced)
- 100 g flour-boiling potatoes(diced)
- 1 carrot (diced)
- 1 onion (chopped)
- 1 clove of garlic (sliced)
- 30 g butter (2 tbsp)
- 1 tbsp honey
- 750 ml vegetable broth
- Salt & pepper to taste
- 2 slices whole-grain baguette(or toasted bread cubes)
- 150 ml milk
- 60 g sour cream  or Crème Fraiche (4 tbsp)
- A splash of lemon juice

## *Preparation:*

1. Cut the baguette into cubes. Heat the remaining butter in a frying pan and fry the bread cubes until crispy. Rest them onto the kitchen paper to use for later.
2. Put everything into your soup maker except milk and sour cream.
3. Please check the Max and Min lines and adjust the fluid accordingly. Don't exceed the maximum limit; keep the fluid between the minimum and maximum levels.
4. Set your soup maker to a "Smooth" setting.
5. Once cooked, add milk and sour cream to your soup and blend it for 10 seconds until it is smooth.
6. Season to taste

# Cauliflower Soup with Rice and Potatoes

- Cooking time: 30 min
- Serves: 2-4
- Diet: Vegetarian, Vegan, Low-Calories

## *Ingredients:*

- 400 gr Potatoes (small cubes)
- 400 gr Cauliflower florets (cut into medium size)
- 1 onion (chopped)
- 1 carrot(grated)
- ½ cup of rice (washed)
- 300 gr canned or frozen peas.
- 900 ml of water.
- 2 vegetable cubes
- Parsley (for garnishing)
- A pinch of ground black pepper &salt to taste.

## *Preparation:*

1. Sauté onion in a pan for 4 minutes and then transfer it to your soup maker. You may want to cook the onions. If you have the "sauté" option in your soup maker.
2. Add all the ingredients to the sauteed onions in your soup maker except parsley.
3. Please check the Max and Min lines and adjust the fluid accordingly. Don't exceed the maximum limit; keep the fluid between the minimum and maximum levels.
4. Set your soup maker to a "Chunky" setting.
5. Once cooked, season to taste.
6. Serve hot with some parsley on top

# Spicy Soup with Mackerel Fillets

- Cooking time: 30 min
- Serves: 2

## *Ingredients:*

- 300 g small cauliflower (1 small cauliflower)
- 1 large potato (cut into small size)
- 1 clove of garlic (chopped)
- 1 onion (chopped)
- 1 tbsp olive oil
- 1 tbsp Thai red curry paste
- 500 ml classic vegetable broth
- 200 ml coconut milk
- Salt & Pepper
- 150 g smoked mackerel fillet flakes (cooked, shredded)
- ½ teaspoon sesame oil

## *Preparation:*

1. Sauté garlic and onion in olive oil on medium heat until translucent in a saucepan.
2. Add Thai Red curry paste and stir fry until the paste is fragrant (If your soup maker has the "Sauté" option, use that instead)
3. Transfer the sauteed ingredients to the soup maker.
4. Add all the ingredients except single cream, smoked mackerel fillets and sesame oil.
5. Please check the Max and Min lines and adjust the fluid accordingly. Don't exceed the maximum limit; keep the fluid between the minimum and maximum levels.
6. Set your soup maker to a "Smooth" setting.
7. Once cooked, add single cream and give it a good stir.
8. Add shredded mackerel fillets and drizzle over with sesame oil.
9. Season to taste and serve hot.

# Creamy Rocket Soup with Parmesan

- Cooking time: 20 min
- Serves: 2-4
- Diet: Vegetarian

## *Ingredients:*

- 2 large potatoes (diced)
- 2 shallots (chopped)
- 1 clove of garlic (sliced)
- 750 ml classic vegetable broth
- 200 ml single cream
- 240-300 g rocket (Arugula) (3 bunches-save some for garnishing)
- Salt and pepper to taste
- 30 g parmesan (grated) (save some for garnishing)

## *Preparation:*

1. Put everything into your soup maker except single cream. (You may want to saute the onion & garlic with 1 tablespoon of vegetable oil, but it is totally up to you)
2. Please check the Max and Min lines and adjust the fluid accordingly. Don't exceed the maximum limit; keep the fluid between the minimum and maximum levels.
3. Set your soup maker to a "Smooth" setting.
4. Once cooked, add single cream to your soup and stir.
5. Season to taste.
6. Grate some parmesan on top of each bowl and add some rocket leaves for garnishing
7. Serve hot.

# Courgette Soup with Yoghurt

- Preparation: 40 min
- Servings 4
- Diet: Vegetarian

## *Ingredients:*

- 800 g courgettes (4 courgettes/ a.k.a zucchinis)
- 200 g leek (1 stick)
- 2 garlic cloves
- 2 branches thyme
- 1 ½ tbsp olive oil
- 800 ml classic vegetable broth
- Salt, Pepper & Cayenne pepper to taste
- 1 ½ tsp white balsamic vinegar
- 1 tbsp sunflower seeds (for garnishing)
- A pinch of paprika powder (sweet)
- 150 g yoghurt (plain)
- 1 tsp runny honey

## *Preparation:*

- Put everything into your soup maker except yoghurt, honey and sunflower seeds.
- Please check the Max and Min lines and adjust the fluid accordingly. Don't exceed the maximum limit; keep the fluid between the minimum and maximum levels.
- Set your soup maker to a "Smooth" setting.
- Once cooked, add yoghurt and honey to your soup and stir it well.
- Season with salt, pepper, and cayenne pepper (start with a pinch of cayenne pepper as it is hot).

  Optional: Serve Cold... Let it cool down and chill in the fridge for 30 minutes to 1 hour if you prefer cold. It is a perfect summer soup.

# Carrot Soup with Orange and Chilli

- Cooking time: 20 min
- Serves: 4
- Diet: Vegetarian, Vegan, Low Calorie

## *Ingredients:*

- 5 carrots (grated)
- 2 medium onions (chopped finely)
- 3 medium potatoes (diced into small cubes)
- ¼ teaspoon dried thyme
- 750 ml water
- 2 vegetable cubes
- 80 g red lentils
- Juice of 1 orange
- 1 tablespoon orange zest (optional/ for garnishing)
- A pinch of Chilli powder (season to desired strength later on)
- Salt and pepper to taste

## *Preparation:*

1. Put all the ingredients into your soup maker except the orange zest and chilli powder.
2. Please check the Max and Min lines and adjust the fluid accordingly. Don't exceed the maximum limit and keep the fluid between the minimum and maximum levels.
3. Set your soup maker to a "Smooth" setting.
4. Once cooked, blend it for 10 seconds intervals until it is smooth.
5. Season to taste and add more chilli powder if you want to and give it a good stir.
6. Add orange zest if you like to use it; you can sprinkle it on each bowl.
7. Serve hot.

# Tomato Coconut Soup with Prawns

- Cooking time: 25min
- Serves 2

## *Ingredients:*

- 200 ml orange juice
- 140 g prawns (cooked)
- 1 pinch of cayenne pepper
- 400 g passata
- 200ml coconut milk (1/2 a can)
- 400 ml classic vegetable broth
- 1 spring onion (to garnish -chopped or sliced)
- Salt and pepper to taste

## *Preparation:*

1. Put everything into your soup maker except spring onion.
2. Please check the Max and Min lines and adjust the fluid accordingly. Don't exceed the maximum limit and keep the fluid between the minimum and maximum levels.
3. Set your soup maker to a "Chunky" setting.
4. Once cooked, season to taste. Be easy on cayenne pepper if you don't like it too spicy.
5. Serve in a bowl with chopped spring onions on top.

# Potato Mince Soup with Mushrooms

- Cooking time: 30 min
- Serves: 2-4

## *Ingredients:*

- 600 g a can of baby potatoes
- 200 g leek (1 small stick)
- 800 ml vegetable broth
- 1 tablespoon butter/ghee/ vegetable oil
- Salt & Pepper to taste
- ½ tsp ground cumin
- 200 g mushrooms (a can -drained)
- 400 g ground beef (pre-cooked or raw)
- ½ tsp dried marjoram
- 200 g single cream
- 20 g parsley (to garnish)
- 40 g walnuts (chopped- to garnish)

## *Preparation:*

1. Put all the ingredients into your soup maker except the butter, mincemeat, parsley and walnuts.
2. Please check the Max and Min lines and adjust the fluid accordingly. Don't exceed the maximum limit and keep the fluid between the minimum and maximum levels.
3. Set your soup maker to a "Smooth" setting.
4. While your soup is cooking, If the mincemeat is raw: Heat a tablespoon of butter in a saucepan and cook the mincemeat until it is brown. Drain excess water and oil and set it aside.
5. Once your soup is cooked, add the cream and cooked mincemeat and give it a good stir.
6. Season to taste.
7. Serve soup garnished with parsley and walnuts.

# Tomato and Pepper Soup

- Cooking time: 30
- Serves: 4 -6
- Diet: Vegan, Vegetarian

## *Ingredients:*

- 10-12 salad tomatoes ( riped- any choices, approx. 750 gr)
- 3 bell peppers
- 1 medium onion (chopped)
- 4 clove (s) of garlic
- 500 ml tomato juice
- Salt and Pepper to taste
- A splash of tabasco red (optional)

## *Preparation:*

1. Put all the ingredients into your soup maker.
2. Please check the Max and Min lines and adjust the fluid accordingly. Don't exceed the maximum limit and keep the fluid between the minimum and maximum levels.
3. Choose the "Smooth" setting and blend the ingredients until smooth.
4. Once cooked, season to taste; add a tabasco splash.
5. Serve with mint/parsley on top for garnishing (optional)

# Easy and Lazy Beetroot Soup

- Cooking time: 30 min
- Serves: 4-6
- Diet: Vegetarian, Vegan

## *Ingredients:*

- 500 g pre-cooked beetroot (cut into chunky size)
- 100 g celeriac (diced into small cubes)
- Salt and pepper to taste
- 1 tablespoon sugar
- 2 tablespoon tomato paste
- 1/4 teaspoon cumin
- 2 bay leaves
- ¼ teaspoon allspice
- 3 garlic gloves
- 1 lemon juice
- 2 vegetables/ or chicken cubes
- 1 l water
- A dollop of sour cream (to garnish-Optional))
- Half a bunch of shredded parsley (to garnish)

## *Preparation:*

1. Put all the ingredients into your soup maker except salt, pepper, sour cream(vegetarian option) and parsley.
2. Please check the Max and Min lines and adjust the fluid accordingly. Don't exceed the maximum limit; keep the fluid between the minimum and maximum levels.
3. Choose the "Chunky" setting and cook until the required time.
4. Season to taste with salt and pepper.
5. Serve with a dollop of sour cream and parsley on top.

# Simply Delicious Mushroom Soup

- Cooking time: 30 min
- Serves: 4-6

## *Ingredients:*

- 300 g peeled mushrooms cut into thick slices
- 2 chopped leeks or 3 chopped fresh onions
- 2 cloves garlic
- A little fresh oregano or thyme
- 700 ml chicken broth or vegetable broth
- 2-3 tablespoons olive oil
- Sour cream or strained yoghurt for serving (optional)
- Salt & ground pepper to taste

## *Preparation:*

1. Put all the ingredients into your soup maker.
2. Please check the Max and Min lines and adjust the fluid accordingly. Don't exceed the maximum limit; keep the fluid between the minimum and maximum levels.
3. Choose the "Smooth" setting and blend the ingredients until smooth.
4. Once cooked, season to taste;
5. Serve hot with a warm toasted baguette.

# Super Easy Yogurt Soup

- Preparation: 20 min
- Serves: 2-4
- Diet: Vegetarian, Low Calories

## *Ingredients:*

- 500 g fat-free yoghurt
- 1 egg
- 1 l water
- 2 tablespoons of flour
- Salt & pepper to taste
- ½ teaspoon dried mint

## *Preparation:*

1. Put yoghurt, egg, flour, salt&pepper and dried mint into a bowl and whisk it well.
2. Decant the mixture to your soup maker.
3. Add 1 l water.
4. Please check the Max and Min lines and adjust the fluid accordingly. Don't exceed the maximum limit; keep the fluid between the minimum and maximum levels.
5. Set your soup maker to the "Smooth" setting.
6. Once cooked, season to taste and add more dried mint if you prefer.
7. Serve hot with some dried mints on top for garnishing.

# Creamy Radish Soup

- Preparation:25-30 min
- Serves: 2-4
- Diet: Vegetarian

## *Ingredients:*

- 10 radishes with leaves (diced, small cubes)
- 150 g floury potatoes (diced, small cubes)
- 1 tablespoon vegetable oil
- 1 shallot (chopped)
- 900 ml vegetable broth
- 200 g low fat creme fraiche cheese
- A pinch of salt & Pepper
- 1/8 teaspoon nutmeg

## *Preparation:*

1. Put all the ingredients into your soup maker except soft cheese. (You may want to saute the onion, radishes and potato with 1 tablespoon of vegetable oil, but it is totally up to you)
2. Please check the Max and Min lines and adjust the fluid accordingly. Don't exceed the maximum limit and keep the fluid between the minimum and maximum levels.
3. Set your soup maker to a "Smooth" setting.
4. Once cooked, make sure the soup is smooth; if not, blend it for 10 seconds until it is smooth.
5. Add Crème Fraiche and give it a good stir.
6. Season to taste and serve it with warm bread.

# One-Pot Tomato Soup

- Cooking time:20 min
- Serves: 2-4
- Calories: Vegetarian, Vegan

## *Ingredients:*

- 2 poles of celery
- 1 clove of garlic
- Sea-salt to taste
- 800 g tomatoes (chopped) or passata
- 1 tbsp olive oil
- 1 tbsp tomato paste
- 800 ml vegetable broth
- 1 pinch sugar
- 1 pinch of lemon peel
- Freshly ground pepper
- 1 tbsp fresh parsley (to garnish)

## *Preparation:*

1. Put all the ingredients into your soup maker.
2. Please check the Max and Min lines and adjust the fluid accordingly. Don't exceed the maximum limit and keep the fluid between the minimum and maximum levels.
3. Set your soup maker to a "Smooth" setting.
4. Once cooked, blend it for 10 seconds intervals until it is smooth.
5. Season to taste.
6. Serve with some fresh parsley on top.

# Quick Broccoli Soup

- Cooking Time: 30 min
- Serves: 2-4
- Diet: Vegetarian, Low-calorie

## *Ingredients:*

- 800 g broccoli (approx. 2-3, cut into small sizes)
- 1 leek (chopped)
- 1 medium-size potato (cut into small sizes)
- 1 tablespoon vegetable oil
- 200 ml light cream
- Salt and black pepper to taste

## *Preparation:*

1. Put all the ingredients into your soup maker except the light cream.
2. Please check the Max and Min lines and adjust the fluid accordingly. Don't exceed the maximum limit and keep the fluid between the minimum and maximum levels.
3. Set your soup maker to a "Smooth" setting.
4. Once cooked, add cream to your soup and stir it.
5. Season to taste.
6. Serve hot.

# Easy Chicken Soup

- Preparation: 20 min
- Serves: 2-4
- Diet: Low Calorie

## *Ingredients:*

- Cooked chicken thighs or breasts ( approx.. 400g)
- 2 small onions chopped
- 2 tablespoons plain flour
- Salt & Pepper to taste
- 100 ml light single cream or skimmed milk
- 1 l classic chicken broth (or 2 chicken cubes dissolved)

## *Preparation:*

1. Put all the ingredients into your soup maker except cream. (You may want to saute the onion and garlic with 1 tablespoon of vegetable oil and add flour to the pan, but this process is totally up to you. You may add everything to the soup maker and forget about it)
2. Please check the Max and Min lines and adjust the fluid accordingly. Don't exceed the maximum limit and keep the fluid between the minimum and maximum levels.
3. Set your soup maker to a "Smooth" setting.
4. Once cooked, add single light cream and stir it well.
5. Season to taste

# Effortless Asian Spicy Lentil Soup

- Preparation: 25 min
- Serves: 2-6
- Diet: Vegetarian, Low calories

## *Ingredients:*

- 300 g red lentils
- 1 l water
- 2 vegetable cubes
- 1 medium onion (chopped)
- ½ tablespoon curry powder
- 2 celery sticks (diced)
- Salt and pepper to taste
- 4 tbsp fat-free yoghurt
- 1 spring coriander(to garnish)

## *Preparation :*

1. Put all the ingredients into your soup maker except yoghurt.
2. Please check the Max and Min lines and adjust the fluid accordingly. Don't exceed the maximum limit and keep the fluid between the minimum and maximum levels.
3. Set your soup maker to a "Smooth" setting.
4. Once cooked, add yoghurt to the soup and stir it well.
5. Taste the soup and add curry powder to taste If necessary.
6. Season and serve it in a bowl with some coriander on top.

# Curried Brussels Sprouts Soup

- Preparation: 30 min
- Serves: 2-4
- Diet: Vegetarian, Low Calorie, Seasonal

## *Ingredients:*

- 600 g fresh brussels sprouts (halved)
- 2 cm fresh ginger (sliced thinly)
- 1 small onion (chopped)
- 600 ml vegetable broth
- 200 ml of low-fat coconut milk can
- 2 teaspoons of curry powder
- Salt and pepper to taste
- 2 tbsp lemon juice

## *Preparation:*

1. Heat the oil in a saucepan and sauté the Brussels sprouts with the onions and ginger for five minutes. If your soup maker has a "sauté" option, use that instead of a saucepan.
2. Put all the ingredients into your soup maker except lemon juice.
3. Please check the Max and Min lines and adjust the fluid accordingly. Don't exceed the maximum limit; keep the fluid between the minimum and maximum levels.
4. Set your soup maker to a "Chunky " setting. You can always blend it later if you prefer smooth.
5. Once cooked, season to taste and drizzle some lemon juice over the bowl.
6. Perfect company of turkey club sandwich during the Christmas holiday.

# Mixed Beans Soup with Sweet Potatoes

- Cooking Time: 30 min
- Serves: 2-4
- Diet: Vegetarian, Vegan

## *Ingredients:*

- 250 g sweet potatoes (diced)
- A can of mixed beans (pre-cooked, drained, net weight 270 g)
- 10 g carrot (diced)
- 1 small onion (chopped)
- 750 ml vegetable stock
- 2 celery stalks (chopped)
- 2 garlic (sliced)
- Salt and pepper to taste
- ¼ teaspoon paprika
- ¼ teaspoon dried oregano

## *Preparation:*

1. Put all the ingredients into your soup maker.
2. Please check the Max and Min lines and adjust the fluid accordingly. Don't exceed the maximum limit; keep the water between the minimum and maximum levels.
3. Set your soup maker to a "Chunky" setting.
4. Season to taste.

# Turmeric Stew

- Cooking time: 25-30 minutes
- Serves: 2-4
- Diet: Low calorie

## *Ingredients:*

- 400 g pre-cooked chicken (diced)
- 1 spring onion (chopped)
- 1 red pepper (diced)
- 3 medium carrots (chopped)
- 200 g peas(fresh or frozen)
- 3 celery stalks (chopped)
- 1 tbsp coconut oil
- 1 tbsp turmeric (powder)
- 1 tsp cumin (powder)
- 750 ml chicken broth
- Salt and pepper to taste

## *Preparation:*

1. Put all the ingredients into your soup maker
2. Please check the Max and Min lines and adjust the fluid accordingly. Don't exceed the maximum limit, and keep the fluid levels between the minimum and maximum.
3. Set your soup maker to the "Chunky" setting.
4. Once cooked, season to taste with salt and pepper.

# Vermicelli Soup

- Cooking time: 25-30 minutes
- Serves: 2-4

## *Ingredients:*

- 1 tbsp butter
- 250 g vermicelli (broken)
- 2 tbsp tomato puree (diluted in 100 ml water)
- 1 shallot(chopped)
- 1 chopped garlic
- 1 tsp olive oil
- A pinch of salt and pepper
- 1 l chicken or vegetable stock
- 1 tbsp dried mint
- A splash of Worcestershire sauce to taste (for seasoning)
- 1 stem flat-leaf parsley (to garnish)

## *Preparation:*

1. Put all the ingredients into your soup maker. (You may want to sauté the shallot and garlic with 1 tablespoon of butter, but it is totally up to you)
2. Please check the Max and Min lines and adjust the fluid levels accordingly.
3. Set your soup maker to the "Chunky" setting.
4. Once cooked, season the soup with Worcestershire sauce, salt, and pepper.
5. Drizzle with olive oil and more mint as desired.

# Italian-Style Tomato Soup

- Cooking Time: 30 min
- Serves: 2-4
- Diet: Vegetarian, Vegan

## *Ingredients:*

- 2 cans of chopped tomatoes (or 800 gr passata)
- 1 onion chopped
- 2-3 cloves of garlic
- 4 tbsp olive oil
- 1 tsp oregano or Italian herbs
- 750 ml water
- 2 vegetable cubes
- 2 teaspoon tomato paste
- A pinch of salt & pepper
- Half a bunch of basil (chopped)
- ½ tsp balsamic vinegar (for seasoning)

## *Preparation:*

1. Sauté the onion and garlic with 1 tablespoon of vegetable oil in a saucepan until they are translucent.
2. Decant everything in the saucepan to your soup maker. Add the rest of the ingredients.
3. Please check the Max and Min lines and adjust the fluid levels accordingly. Don't exceed the maximum limit; keep the fluid level between the minimum and maximum.
4. Set your soup maker to a "Smooth" setting.
5. Once cooked, season to taste with salt and pepper.
6. Scatter the chopped basil on top and mix in a portion.
7. Drizzle olive oil onto the soup and serve immediately.

# Creamy Vegan Carrot and Parsnip Soup

- Cooking time: 25 min
- Serves: 2-4
- Diet: Vegan, Vegetarian

## *Ingredients:*

- 10 g ginger (approx. 1 piece sliced)
- 500 g carrots (4 carrots)
- 400 g parsnips
- 1 tbsp olive oil
- 850 ml vegetable broth
- 1 tsp turmeric powder
- ½ tsp ground coriander
- Salt & pepper to taste
- 120 ml almond cream or another vegetable cream substitute
- 30 g hazelnut kernels (2 tbsp)
- 10 g parsley (0.5 bunch)

## *Preparation:*

1. Peel and dice the ginger. Next, clean, peel and chop the carrots and parsnips.
2. Heat the oil in a pot. Sauté the ginger and vegetables in it for 3 minutes over medium heat. If your soup maker has a "Sauté" option, use that option.
3. Pour the broth and season with turmeric, coriander, salt and pepper into your soup maker.
4. Choose the "Smooth" setting.
5. In the meantime, roast the nuts in a hot pan without fat over medium heat for 3 minutes; then roughly chop.
6. Once the soup is cooked, stir in the almond cream.
7. Wash the parsley, shake dry and chop the leaves.
8. Arrange the soup in bowls and serve sprinkled with nuts and parsley

# Potato and Spinach Soup with Blue Cheese

- Cooking time: 25 minutes
- Serves: 2- 4
- Diet: Vegetarian

## *Ingredients:*

- 300 g potatoes
- 250 ml of vegetable stock
- 400 g spinach (frozen)
- 200 ml light single cream
- 100g Blue Cheese, Salt & black pepper to taste
- A pinch of nutmeg (grated/powder)

## *Preparation:*

1. Put all the ingredients into your soup maker except the single cream.
2. Please check the Max and Min lines and adjust the fluid accordingly. Don't exceed the maximum limit; keep the water between the minimum and maximum levels.
3. Set your soup maker to the "Smooth" setting. Add the single cream and stir it well.
4. Season to taste. Add blue cheese crumbles on top.

# Tomato Soup with Chives

- Cooking time: 25 minutes
- Serves: 2- 4
- Diet: Vegetarian, Vegan

## *Ingredients*

- 8-10 medium size tomatoes (chopped)
- 1 large onion (chopped)
- 2 -3 garlic cloves
- 20 g butter
- ½ teaspoon of dried rosemary
- ½ teaspoon of dried thyme
- 700-800 ml vegetable broth
- 1 teaspoon sugar
- Salt & pepper to taste
- Chives for garnishing

## *Preparation:*

1. Put all the ingredients into your soup maker except chives.
2. Please check your soup maker's Max and minimum lines and adjust the fluid levels accordingly. Don't exceed the maximum limit, and keep the fluid level between the minimum and maximum.
3. Set your soup maker to the "Smooth" setting.
4. Once cooked, add sugar, and stir.
5. Taste and season with sugar, salt and pepper if necessary.
6. Pour the soup into pre-warmed cups and serve garnished with chives

# Artichoke Cream Soup

- Cooking time: 30 min
- Serves: 2-6
- Diet: Vegetarian

## *Ingredients:*

- 800 g artichokes
- ½ lemon juice
- 1 onion chopped
- 2 garlic cloves
- 4 tbsp olive oil
- 125 ml dry white wine
- 500 ml classic vegetable broth
- 50 g green olives (without stones)
- 1 tbsp flaked almonds
- 100 ml whipped cream
- Salt & Pepper to taste

## *Preparation:*

1. Heat 3 tablespoons of olive oil in a saucepan. Sauté the onion and garlic until translucent while stirring. Add artichoke pieces and cook for about 3 minutes.
2. Add all the ingredients except olives, almonds and cream.
3. Choose the "Smooth" setting.
4. In the meantime, finely chop the olives and mix them with the remaining olive oil in a small bowl.
5. Roast the almond flakes in a pan until golden yellow; frequently stir, remove, and allow to cool.
6. Once cooked, pour in the cream and season with salt and pepper.
7. Pour into soup bowls.
8. Serve with the almonds and the olive oil mixture.

# Halloween Soup

- Cooking time 30 min
- Serves: 2-4
- Diet: Vegan, Vegetarian

## *Ingredients:*

- 100 g shallots (chopped)
- 300 g pumpkin (diced)
- 1 tbsp olive oil
- 2 tomatoes (chopped)
- 2 tomatoes, dried (chopped)
- 1/2 l chicken stock
- Juice of 1 orange (approx. 200 ml)
- 20 g pickled ginger (for garnishing)
- Salt pepper to taste

## *Preparation:*

1. Heat one tablespoon of olive oil, sauté sliced shallots and pumpkin in olive oil for three minutes in a saucepan.
2. Add the tomatoes, including sun-dried tomatoes and cook for further 3 minutes.
3. Transfer the mixture to your soup maker.
4. Add all the other ingredients to the mixture except pickled ginger.
5. Choose the "Smooth" setting.
6. Once cooked, stir it well and season with salt and pepper.
7. Serve with pickled gingers on top.

# Creamy Fennel Soup with Scallops

- Preparation: 30 min
- Serves: 2-4

## *Ingredients:*

- 1 tuber fennel
- 200 g small potatoes (2 medium potatoes)
- 2 small shallots
- 1 tbsp olive oil
- 800 ml chicken broth
- 1 pinch saffron thread
- 1 bay leaf
- 100ml single cream
- Salt & Pepper to taste

## *For scallops:*

- 4 scallops (ready to cook; with roe)
- 1 tbsp olive oil
- 1 tbsp aniseed liqueur (as desired-Pernod, Sambuca, Ouzo could be used in a small amount )

## *Preparation:*

1. Clean and wash the fennel. Cut off the fennel greens and set them aside. Cut the fennel bulb into 1 cm cubes.
2. Peel, wash and dice the potatoes and chop shallots.
3. Heat 1 tablespoon of olive oil in a saucepan and fry the shallots until translucent. Add the fennel and potatoes and sauté briefly.
4. Transfer the mixture to the soup maker. Add the stock, saffron and bay leaf.
5. Choose the setting "Smooth".
6. While the soup is cooking, season the scallops with salt and pepper.
7. Heat the remaining oil in a non-stick pan and fry the mussels for 45 seconds on each side.

8. Deglaze with aniseed liqueur to taste and remove from heat.
9. Once the soup is cooked, remove the bay leaf and choose the "Blend" option to puree the soup very finely with your soup maker.
10. Add the cream and stir it well.
11. Season to taste with salt and pepper.
12. Serve the soup with glazed scallops.

# Asparagus Soup

- Cooking time 30 min
- Serves: 2-4
- Diet: Vegetarian

## *Ingredients:*

- 350 g green asparagus (chopped)
- 1 shallot (chopped)
- 10 g butter (1 tbsp)
- 600 ml classic vegetable broth
- 30 g parmesan (1 piece- grated)
- ½ lemon juice
- 100 ml double cream
- Salt & Pepper to taste

## *Preparation:*

1. Wash and drain the asparagus and cut off any woody ends. Peel the asparagus in the lower third. Cut the sticks into pieces about 2 cm long.
2. Peel and finely chop shallot.
3. Heat the butter in a saucepan. Sauté the asparagus pieces and shallot over medium heat.
4. Transfer the mixture to your soup maker and add the remaining ingredients except for the cream.
5. Please check the fluid levels of your soup maker, add if necessary
6. Choose the "Smooth" setting.
7. Once cooked, grate the parmesan finely.
8. Add the parmesan and the cream to the asparagus soup and stir it well.
9. Season with salt, pepper, and a little lemon juice.
10. Serve hot with toasted sourdough bread.

# Watercress Soup

- Cooking Time: 20-30 min
- Calories: 230 kcal
- Servings 2

## *Ingredients:*

- 2 shallots
- 100 g small floury potatoes
- 1 tbsp olive oil
- 600 ml vegetable broth
- 100 ml soy cream
- 250 g watercress
- Salt & Pepper
- Cooked Trout fillets or Mackerel fillets cut(-optional)

## *Preparation:*

1. Peel and finely chop shallots.
2. Peel the potatoes, rinse, drain and cut into small cubes.
3. Heat the oil in a heavy saucepan. Sauté shallots and potatoes in it for about 1 minute until colourless.
4. Pour in the vegetable stock and watercress and bring to a boil.
5. Transfer the mixture to your soup maker
6. Please check the fluid levels of your soup maker, and add more fluid if necessary.
7. Choose the "Smooth" setting.
8. Once cooked, add soy cream and stir it well.
9. Season the soup with salt and pepper. Cut 50-80 gr smoked trout fillet/ mackerel into pieces (optional).
10. Put the soup on pre-warmed deep plates and serve the fillet pieces on top.

# Miso Soup

- Cooking Time: 20-30 min
- Calories: 230 kcal
- Servings 2

## *Ingredients:*

- 400 g cooked chicken breast fillet (2 chicken breast fillets)
- 30 g ginger (1 piece) sliced
- 1 tbsp sesame oil
- 4 tbsp teriyaki sauce
- 4 spring onions- chopped
- 2 tbsp sesame
- salt
- pepper
- 1 l chicken broth
- 40 g miso paste
- 2 tbsp light soy sauce
- 1 boiled egg (optional)

## *Preparation:*

1. Put all the ingredients into your soup maker except chives.
2. Please check your soup maker's maximum and minimum lines and adjust the fluid levels accordingly. Don't exceed the maximum limit, and keep the fluid level between the minimum and maximum.
3. Set your soup maker to the "Chunky" setting.
4. Once cooked, stir it well. Season it with soy sauce and sprinkle with sesame seeds. The finished miso soup can now be served.
5. Pour the soup into pre-warmed cups and serve garnished with a boiled egg.

# Pumpkin and Ginger Soup

- Cooking time 15 to 30 min
- Servings: 4
- Diet: Vegetarian, Vegan, Low calorie

## Ingredients:

- 1 kg of pumpkin diced
- 1 pc onion diced
- 12 g ginger (fresh) chopped
- 1 tbsp olive oil
- 500 ml of water
- 1 can (s) of coconut milk (400 gr)
- 1 pinch of turmeric
- 1 teaspoon cumin
- salt
- pepper

## Preparation:

1. For the pumpkin ginger soup, cut the onion into small pieces, peel the ginger and chop it up. Peel and core the pumpkin and cut it into small pieces.
2. Put everything in your soup maker and add the onion and ginger.
3. Add a pinch of turmeric and cumin.
4. Then add the pumpkin and water.
5. Pour in the coconut milk and
6. Set your soup maker to a "smooth" setting.
7. Once cooked, puree the whole thing until it is smooth.
8. Season the finished pumpkin ginger soup with salt and pepper.
9. Serve hot with some goat cheese and sourdough bread (optional)

# Potato Soup with Emmenthal Cheese

- Cooking time 30 min
- Servings: 4
- Diet: Vegetarian, Winter Warme

## *Ingredients:*

- 400 g potatoes thin sliced
- 2 onions (large) diced
- 2 clove (s) of garlic chopped
- some clarified butter (for frying)
- 150 g Appenzeller (Emmental or Gruyere as substitute)
- 1500 ml of vegetable stock
- 1 dash of white vinegar
- salt
- pepper
- 1 bunch of chives
- 1 bay leaf
- 1 sprig (s) of thyme
- 1 tsp Caraway seeds (whole or ground, as desired)

## *Preparation:*

1. Put all the ingredients into your soup maker except chives.
2. Please check your soup maker's maximum and minimum lines and adjust the fluid levels accordingly. Don't exceed the maximum limit, and keep the fluid level between the minimum and maximum.
3. Set your soup maker to the "Smooth" setting.
4. Once cooked, stir it well. Season if necessary.
5. Pour the soup into pre-warmed cups and serve with a toasted baguette and relish.

# Fast Fish Soup with Vegetables

- Cooking time: 20-30 minutes
- Servings: 2- 4

## *Ingredients:*

- 2 red pepper sliced
- 200 g small carrots (2 large carrots) thinly sliced
- 1 shallot diced
- 1 tsp rapeseed oil
- salt
- pepper
- 1 l fish stock
- 350 g haddock fillet- cut into small pieces
- Worcester sauce to taste
- 1 stem flat-leaf parsley (for garnish)

## *Preparation:*

1. Put all the ingredients into your soup maker except parsley and Worcestershire sauce.
2. Please check your soup maker's maximum and minimum lines and adjust the fluid levels accordingly. Don't exceed the maximum limit, and keep the fluid level between the minimum and maximum.
3. Set your soup maker to the "Chunky" setting
4. Once cooked, season if necessary.
5. Add some Worcestershire sauce to taste and garnish it with parsley on top.

# Creamy Chives Soup

- Cooking time: 30 min
- Servings: 2

## *Ingredients*

- 150 g Chives
- 600ml vegetable stock
- 150 ml single cream
- salt
- pepper
- a pinch of Nutmeg (ground)

## *Preparation:*

- Put all the ingredients into your soup maker.
- Please check your soup maker's maximum and minimum lines and adjust the fluid levels accordingly. Don't exceed the maximum limit, and keep the fluid level between the minimum and maximum.
- Set your soup maker to the "Smooth" setting.
- Once cooked, stir it well. Season if necessary.
- Pour the soup into cups and serve it with warm pita bread and feta cheese.

# Sauerkraut Soup

- Cooking time: 30 min
- Servings: 4

## *Ingredients:*

- 2 Red peppers sliced
- 2 Onions - diced
- 2 tbsp coconut oil
- 2 teaspoons of caraway seeds
- 1 tbsp paprika powder
- 1.5 l vegetable broth
- 500 ml sauerkraut
- 300 g cooked corned beef
- 1 pinch (s) of salt and pepper

## *Preparation:*

1. Put all the ingredients into your soup maker.
2. Please check your soup maker's maximum and minimum lines and adjust the fluid levels accordingly. Don't exceed the maximum limit, and keep the liquid level between the minimum and maximum.
3. Set your soup maker to the "Chunky" setting.
4. Once cooked, Season and serve hot.

# Kale Soup

- Cooking time: 25 min
- Servings: 4

## *Ingredients:*

- 600 g of kale chopped
- 0.5 Chinese cabbage or savoy cabbage chopped
- 3 handfuls of spinach
- 1 green onion chopped
- 3 cloves of garlic
- 2 tbsp olive oil
- 300 ml beef stock
- 100 ml coconut milk
- 1 teaspoon nutmeg
- 1 teaspoon salt and pepper
- 1 teaspoon mustard (optional)

## *Preparation:*

1. Put all the ingredients into your soup maker.
2. Please check your soup maker's maximum and minimum lines and adjust the fluid levels accordingly. Don't exceed the maximum limit and keep the liquid level between the minimum and maximum.
3. Set your soup maker to the "Smooth" setting.
4. Once cooked, season if necessary.
5. If you want, add a dollop of mustard to the soup before serving.
6. Serve hot with some toasted baguette and sliced goat cheese.

# Onion Soup

- Cooking time: 25 min
- Servings: 4
- Diet: Vegetarian, Vegan and Low Calorie

## *Ingredients:*

- 450 g onions sliced (3 large onions)
- 2 cloves of garlic chopped
- 1.5 l vegetable stock or just water
- 200 ml white wine (optional)
- 2 bay leaves
- 15 peppercorns
- 10 mustard seeds
- 10 juniper berries
- 1 pinch (s) of salt, pepper
- 1 tbsp olive oil

## *Preparation:*

1. Peel the onions cut them in half, and cut them into very thin strips. Peel the garlic cloves and cut them into small pieces.
2. Heat a little olive oil in a large saucepan, and fry the onions and garlic until golden until the onions are soft. If necessary, deglaze with the white wine and add the vegetable stock/water.
3. Pour the spices into a tea infuser or sachet.
4. Decant the ingredients in the saucepan into your soup maker and add a spice sachet.
5. Please check your soup maker's maximum and minimum lines and adjust the fluid levels accordingly. Don't exceed the maximum limit and keep the liquid level between the minimum and maximum.
6. Close the lid.
7. Set your soup maker to the "Chunky" setting.
8. Then remove the spices and, if necessary, season again with pepper and salt.

# Immune Booster Soup

- Cooking time: 25 min
- Servings: 4

## *Ingredients:*

- 800 ml beef broth
- 1 onion chopped
- 1 small broccoli head
- 2 handfuls of shiitake mushrooms
- 1 thumb-sized piece of ginger sliced
- 1 teaspoon turmeric powder
- Salt to taste

## *Preparation:*

1. Put all the ingredients into your soup maker.
2. Please check your soup maker's maximum and minimum lines and adjust the fluid levels accordingly. Don't exceed the maximum limit and keep the fluid level between the minimum and maximum.
3. Set your soup maker to the "Smooth" setting.
4. Once cooked, season if necessary.
5. Serve hot with some toast.
   Perfect breakfast for cold winter mornings

# Mulligatawny Soup

- Cooking time: 30 min
- Servings: 4

## *Ingredients:*

- 20g ghee
- 2 tbsp olive oil
- 1 tbsp tomato purée
- 1 tsp ground cumin
- 1 apple chopped
- 1 potato, peeled and chopped
- 1 onion, finely chopped
- 3 carrots chopped
- 2 garlic cloves, chopped
- 1-inch ginger, peeled and grated
- 2 tbsp medium curry powder
- 1/2 tsp chilli powder
- 1.2l chicken stock
- ½ lemon, juiced
- ½ small bunch of coriander, shredded
- Boiled rice (to serve)

## *Preparation:*

1. Put all the ingredients into your soup maker.
2. Please check your soup maker's maximum and minimum lines and adjust the fluid levels accordingly. Don't exceed the maximum limit and keep the fluid level between the minimum and maximum.
3. Set your soup maker to the "Smooth" setting.
4. Once cooked, season if necessary.
5. Serve hot with some boiled rice and naan bread.

# Chicken and Vegetable Soup

- Cooking time: 30 min
- Servings: 4

## *Ingredients:*

- 600 g of white potatoes diced
- 500 g of carrots chopped
- 450 g of leek chopped
- 250 g of frozen peas
- 1, 5 l Vegetable stock
- Salt & Pepper
- 400g cooked chicken shredded.

## *Preparation:*

1. Put all the ingredients into your soup maker.
2. Please check your soup maker's maximum and minimum lines and adjust the fluid levels accordingly. Don't exceed the maximum limit and keep the fluid level between the minimum and maximum.
3. Set your soup maker to the "Chunky" setting.
4. Once cooked, season if necessary.
5. Serve hot with toasted country bread

# Christmas Brussels Sprouts Soup

- Cooking time: 30 min
- Servings: 2
- Diet: Vegan, Vegetarian, Seasonal

## *Ingredients:*

- 400 g Brussels sprouts
- 1 onion
- 1 clove of garlic
- 1 tbsp coconut oil
- 500 ml vegetable stock
- 1 teaspoon salt
- 1/2 tsp pepper
- 1 pinch (s) of nutmeg
- 100 ml coconut milk

## *Preparation:*

1. Put all the ingredients into your soup maker.
2. Please check your soup maker's maximum and minimum lines and adjust the fluid levels accordingly. Don't exceed the maximum limit and keep the fluid level between the minimum and maximum.
3. Set your soup maker to the "Smooth" setting.
4. Once cooked, season if necessary.

# Country Farm Potato Soup

- Cooking time: 30 min
- Servings: 4

## *Ingredients:*

- 6 potatoes
- 1 onion chopped
- 1 tbsp olive oil
- 2 fennels
- 700 ml bone broth/ beef broth
- 1 tbsp hot mustard
- 4 slices of bacon
- 2 spring onions
- 1 teaspoon nutmeg spice
- 1 pinch (s) of salt

## *Preparation:*

1. Peel and roughly dice the potatoes and onions.
2. Halve the fennel, remove the stalk in a wedge shape and cut roughly into strips.
3. Put potatoes, broth, and fennels into your soup maker.
4. Please check your soup maker's maximum and minimum lines and adjust the fluid levels accordingly. Don't exceed the maximum limit and keep the fluid level between the minimum and maximum.
5. Set your soup maker to the "Smooth" setting.
6. Take out the bacon. While the soup is cooking, fry the bacon in a pan without fat until crispy. Cut the spring onions into rings and fry them in the bacon fat in the pan. Cut the bacon into strips.
7. Once the soup is cooked, Season to taste with mustard, nutmeg and salt and pepper.
8. Sprinkle with bacon and spring onions before serving.

# Parsnip Soup

- Cooking time: 30 min
- Servings: 2

## *Ingredients*

- 6 parsnips chopped
- 500 ml beef stock
- 1 leek chopped
- 1 onion chopped
- 1 apple chopped
- 150 g bacon
- 2 pinches of salt and pepper
- 1 handful of parsley chopped

## *Preparation:*

1. Put all the ingredients into your soup maker except bacon and parsley.
2. Please check your soup maker's maximum and minimum lines and adjust the fluid levels accordingly. Don't exceed the maximum limit and keep the fluid level between the minimum and maximum.
3. Set your soup maker to the "Smooth" setting.
4. While the soup is cooking, fry the bacon in a pan without fat until crispy. Take out the bacon and cut the bacon into strips.
5. Once cooked, season if necessary.
6. Sprinkle with bacon and parsley before serving.

# Creamy Carrot Soup with Nut Croutons

- Preparation: 10 min
- Ready in 20min
- Servings: 4

## Ingredients

- 500 g carrots
- 400 g sweet potatoes
- 1 tart apple
- 1 onion
- 2 garlic cloves
- 30 g ginger
- 3 tbsp olive oil
- 400 ml coconut milk (can)
- 3 tsp curry powder
- 1 pinch of cinnamon
- salt
- pepper
- 2 wholemeal bread slices
- 3 tbsp walnut kernels
- 2 tbsp lime juice

## Preparation:

1. Wash and chop the carrots. Next, wash, peel and cut the sweet potato and apple. Finally, peel and dice the onion, garlic and ginger.
2. Heat 1 tablespoon of oil in a saucepan. Add onion, garlic, and ginger. Then, sauté over medium heat for 2-3 minutes. Add the carrots, sweet potato and apple and sauté for 2 minutes.
3. Stir coconut milk and set aside 4 tablespoons for the garnish. Pour the carrot mix with the rest of the coconut milk and 500 ml of water.
4. Decant everything and press "Smooth" setting

5. In the meantime, dice the bread and roughly chop the walnuts. Heat the rest of the oil in a pan. Add bread cubes and walnuts. Then, fry for 3–4 minutes until crispy.
6. Choose the "Blend/Puree" option to blitz the carrot soup finely.
7. Season to taste with salt, pepper and lime juice.
8. Garnish the carrot soup with the coconut milk set aside and sprinkle with nut croutons.

# Beetroot soup

- Preparation: 15 min
- ready in 30 min
- servings 4

## Ingredients

- 600 g cooked beetroot
- 3 shallots
- Juice of 2 oranges (approx. 140ml)
- Fillets of 1 orange, cut (optional)
- 2 tbsp rapeseed oil
- 800 ml classic vegetable broth
- 2 stems dill
- 125 ml soy cream
- salt
- pepper

## Preparation:

1. Peel and finely dice the shallots.
2. Squeeze the oranges with a squeezer and leave the juice aside for later.
3. Heat the oil in a saucepan and sauté the shallot cubes over medium heat until translucent.
4. Cut the beetroot into small pieces and add to the pan. Simmer for 2 minutes.
5. Pour in the broth and add all of the orange juice.
6. Transfer the mix in the pan to your soup maker
7. Choose "Chunky" or "Smooth/pureed" setting as your choice
8. In the meantime, wash the dill, shake it dry and pluck the flags off.
9. Once it's cooked, pour in the soy cream.
10. Season with salt and pepper and give it a good stir or blend(for the puree version).
11. Put the beetroot soup in bowls and garnish with the remaining orange fillets (optional) and dill.

# Traditional Chicken Soup

- Preparation: 30 min
- servings 4

## *Ingredients*

- 1 tbsp olive oil
- 2 onions, chopped
- 3 tbsp Greek yoghurt
- 1 garlic clove, crushed
- 3 medium carrots, chopped
- 1 tbsp thyme leaves, roughly chopped
- 1.4l chicken stock
- 300g leftover roast chicken, shredded and skin removed
- a squeeze of lemon juice

## *Preparation:*

1. Put all the ingredients into your soup maker except yoghurt, lemon juice and garlic.
2. Please check your soup maker's maximum and minimum lines and adjust the fluid levels accordingly. Don't exceed the maximum limit and keep the fluid level between the minimum and maximum.
3. Set your soup maker to the "Smooth" setting.
4. Whilst cooking, mix yoghurt, lemon juice and crushed garlic
5. Once the soup is ready, taste and season it if necessary.
6. Add the garlicky yoghurt mixture and stir it well.
7. Serve hot with warm cornbread and olives.

# Apple & Celery Soup

- Preparation: 30 min
- Servings 4

## Ingredients

- 1 medium onion
- 325 g celeriac (1 piece- cut into small pieces)
- 175 g tart apples (1 tart apple)
- 2 tbsp rapeseed oil
- 600 ml classic vegetable broth
- 1 tuber fennel
- salt
- pepper
- 100 ml soy cream

## Preparation:

1. Peel and roughly dice the onion and celery.
2. Peel and quarter the apple, remove the core and also cut the apple into large cubes.
3. Heat half the oil in a large saucepan and sauté the onion cubes for 2-3 minutes over medium heat. Add celery and apple pieces and sauté for 1 minute.
4. Transfer everything to the soup maker.
5. Pour in the stock, and choose the "Smooth" setting.
6. In the meantime, clean, wash and drain the fennel. Finely dice the fennel.
7. Heat a pan, add the remaining oil and roast the fennel cubes over medium heat, stirring, until everything is well browned and soft. Season with salt and pepper and keep warm.
8. Once cooked, Puree/Blend the soup
9. Some soup makers' blender is not so powerful. If the consistency of the soup is lumpy. Then, It is best to strain the soup through a sieve and pour it back into the pot.

10. Add soy cream and heat everything again for about 1 minute.
11. Season the apple and celery soup with salt and pepper, and divide it into preheated soup plates.
12. Serve garnished with roasted fennel.

# Spicy Corn Soup

- Preparation: 15 minutes
- servings 2

## *Ingredients*

- 150 g leek (1 stick)
- 1 green chilli pepper
- 1 clove of garlic
- ½ small lime
- 30 g ginger (1 piece)
- 285 g corn (can; drained weight)
- 1 tbsp rapeseed oil
- 750 ml classic vegetable broth
- 4 stems coriander
- 2 tbsp soy sauce
- Salt & pepper

## *Preparation:*

1. Clean the leek, cut in half lengthways, wash and cut into rings. Wash and clean the chilli pepper and rinse again if necessary.
2. Finely chop the chilli pepper. Peel the garlic and pass it through a press.
3. Wash the lime, and cut it into slices.
4. Peel the ginger and grate finely.
5. Drain the corn in a colander.
6. Heat the oil in a pot. Sauté the leek in it for 1 minute.
7. Add the chilli, garlic, ginger and lime slices and sauté briefly.
8. Transfer everything in the saucepan to the soup maker.
9. Add the stock and the corn, and choose the "Chunky" setting.
10. Wash the coriander, shake dry and chop while the soup is cooking
11. Season the soup with soy sauce, salt and pepper.
12. Sprinkle with the coriander and serve.

# Minestrone Soup

- Preparation: 30 minutes
- Servings: 4

## *Ingredients*

- 3 tbsp olive oil
- 1 onion, finely chopped
- 1 celery stick, finely chopped
- 1 carrot, peeled and finely chopped
- 1 courgette, finely chopped
- 1 large garlic clove, crushed
- ½ tsp dried oregano
- 1 x 400g can of cannellini beans
- 1 x 400g can of diced tomatoes
- 2 tbsp tomato purée
- 1.2 l vegetable stock
- 1 bay leaf
- 70g small pasta
- 100g greens - kale, chard etc.
- Grated Parmesan
- and a handful of basil (for garnishing)

## *Preparation:*

1. Heat 3 tablespoons of oil in a saucepan.
2. Add onion, garlic, and tomato puree. Then, sauté over medium heat for 2-3 minutes.
3. Add the carrots, celery, bay leaf, and courgette. Then, sauté for further 3 minutes.
4. Transfer everything in the saucepan to the soup maker.
5. Add the stock, pasta, greens, and oregano.
6. Choose the "Chunky" setting.
7. Once cooked, season to taste.
8. Add basil and stir it well.
9. Serve it with warm focaccia bread and grated parmesan on top.

# Mixed Vegetable Soup

- Preparation:25 min
- Servings: 4

## *Ingredients:*

- 200 g Wholemeal pasta
- 300 g Carrots diced
- 250 g celery root diced
- 300 g leek sliced
- 250 g Chinese cabbage or kale chopped
- 200 g green pepper diced
- 1 tbsp rapeseed oil
- Salt & Pepper
- 1 ½ l Vegetable broth
- 1 bunch parsley

## *Preparation:*

1. Put all the ingredients into your soup maker.
2. Please check your soup maker's maximum and minimum lines and adjust the fluid levels accordingly. Don't exceed the maximum limit and keep the fluid level between the minimum and maximum.
3. Set your soup maker to the "Chunky" setting.
4. Once the soup is ready, taste and season it if necessary.
5. Serve hot with toasted slices of white bread.

# Beans and Chives Soup

- Cooking Time:     30 min
- Servings: 4
- Diet: Vegan, Vegetarian, Low Calorie

## *Ingredients*

- 400 g drained Cannelini beans (canned)
- 2 bay leaves
- l Vegetable stock
- 100 g chives chopped
- 250 g green asparagus
- tbsp olive oil
- Salt & Pepper
- lemon (juice)

## *Preparation:*

1. Put all the ingredients into your soup maker except asparagus.
2. Please check your soup maker's maximum and minimum lines and adjust the fluid levels accordingly. Don't exceed the maximum limit and keep the fluid level between the minimum and maximum.
3. Set your soup maker to the "Smooth" setting.
4. While your soup is cooking, Heat the oil in a non-stick pan, fry the asparagus over medium heat for about 3 minutes and season with salt.
5. Once the soup is cooked, squeeze a lemon. Season the soup with salt, pepper and a little lemon juice.
6. Serve in portions with the fried asparagus.

# Potato & Carrot Soup with White Asparagus

- Preparation: 30 min
- Servings 2-4

## Ingredients

- small onion
- 20 g ginger (1 piece)
- 400 g carrots (4 carrots)
- 300 g potatoes (4 potatoes)
- tbsp olive oil
- salt
- pepper
- 400 ml classic vegetable broth
- 300 g white asparagus
- orange (juiced)
- stems of basil (for garnishing)

## Preparation:

1. Put all the ingredients into your soup maker except asparagus and orange juice.
2. Please check your soup maker's maximum and minimum lines and adjust the fluid levels accordingly. Don't exceed the maximum limit and keep the fluid level between the minimum and maximum.
3. Set your soup maker to the "Smooth" setting.
4. In the meantime, wash the asparagus, peel it generously and cut off the woody ends. Next, cut the asparagus diagonally into thin slices.
5. Heat the oil in a non-stick pan. Fry the asparagus over medium heat for 6–8 minutes, stirring constantly. Season with salt and pepper.
6. Halve the oranges, squeeze them out and measure out 200-250 ml of juice.
7. Wash the basil, shake dry and pluck the leaves.
8. Once cooked, add the orange juice to the soup and stir it well.

9. Place the potato and carrot soup on deep plates, sprinkle with the asparagus, garnish with basil and serve.

# Tofu Vegetable Pot with Potatoes

- Cooking Time: 25 min
- Servings 2

## *Ingredients:*

- 200 g potatoes (2 potatoes)
- 150 g celeriac (1 piece)
- 100 g carrots (1 carrot)
- 100 g leek (1 small stick)
- 700 ml classic vegetable broth
- 2 bay leaves
- 100 g smoked tofu (Firm) chopped
- nutmeg
- salt
- pepper
- ½ fret chives chopped

## *Preparation:*

1. Peel, wash and dice the potatoes, celery and carrots.
2. Clean the leek, cut lengthways, wash and cut into rings about 1 cm wide.
3. Put all the ingredients into your soup maker.
4. Please check your soup maker's maximum and minimum lines and adjust the fluid levels accordingly. Don't exceed the maximum limit and keep the fluid level between the minimum and maximum.
5. Set your soup maker to the "Chunky" setting.
6. Once the soup is ready, taste and season it if necessary.

# Pea and Ham Soup

- Preparation: 30 min
- Servings 4

## *Ingredients*

- 1 tablespoon of butter
- 1onion, chopped
- 1 medium potato, peeled and diced
- 1 teaspoon English mustard
- 1l ham or pork stock
- 500g frozen petit pois
- 300g shredded ham (cooked)

## *Preparation:*

1. Put all the ingredients into your soup maker except shredded cooked ham.
2. Please check your soup maker's maximum and minimum lines and adjust the fluid levels accordingly. Don't exceed the maximum limit and keep the fluid level between the minimum and maximum.
3. Set your soup maker to the "Smooth" setting.
4. Once cooked, add the shredded ham and give it a good stir.
5. Once the soup is ready, taste and season it if necessary.
6. Best served with toasted bread and some garlic butter.

# Parsnip and Apple Soup

- Preparation: 30 min
- Servings 4

## Ingredients:

- 500 g parsnips
- 750 ml vegetable broth
- 1 onion chopped
- 4 tbsp olive oil
- 1 tsp curry powder
- 1 tbsp wholemeal spelt flour
- 200 g whipped cream
- 1 apple
- 1 bunch chives
- Salt & Pepper
- 4 tsp creme fraiche cheese

## Preparation:

1. Put all the ingredients into your soup maker except flour and crème Fraiche.
2. Mix flour in the 50-100 ml water and add it to the soup maker.
3. Please check your soup maker's maximum and minimum lines and adjust the fluid levels accordingly. Don't exceed the maximum limit and keep the fluid level between the minimum and maximum.
4. Set your soup maker to the "Smooth" setting.
5. Once the soup is ready, taste and season it if necessary.
6. Add crème Fraiche and stir it well.
7. Serve hot with warm sourdough bread and mature cheddar cheese.

# Ginger and Sweet Potato Soup

- Preparation: 30 min
- Servings 4

## Ingredients

- 500 g sweet potatoes
- 200 g carrots
- 2 shallots
- 2 garlic cloves
- 20 g ginger (1 piece) sliced
- 2 tbsp olive oil
- 900 ml vegetable broth
- Salt & Pepper
- 2 tsp curry powder
- 1 tsp turmeric
- 100 g creme fraiche cheese

## Preparation:

1. Put all the ingredients into your soup maker except crème Fraiche.
2. Please check your soup maker's maximum and minimum lines and adjust the fluid levels accordingly. Don't exceed the maximum limit and keep the fluid level between the minimum and maximum.
3. Set your soup maker to the "Smooth" setting.
4. Once the soup is ready, taste and season it if necessary.
5. Add the crème Fraiche and stir it well.
6. Serve hot with naan bread.

# Creamy Potato and Leek Soup

- Preparation: 30 min
- Servings 4

## *Ingredients:*

- 500 g waxy potatoes
- 1-rod leek
- 2 tbsp olive oil
- 800 ml vegetable broth
- 100 ml  double cream
- salt
- pepper
- A pinch of nutmeg

## *Preparation:*

1. Put all the ingredients into your soup maker except double cream
2. Please check your soup maker's maximum and minimum lines and adjust the fluid levels accordingly. Don't exceed the maximum limit and keep the fluid level between the minimum and maximum.
3. Set your soup maker to the "Smooth" setting.
4. Once the soup is ready, taste and season it if necessary.
5. Add the double cream and stir it well.
6. Serve hot with toasted white bread and butter.

# Potato Soup with Mushrooms

- Preparation: 30 min
- Servings 4

## Ingredients

- 800 g potatoes
- 200 g carrots
- 100 g onions
- 2 tbsp butter
- salt
- pepper
- 1 tsp caraway seeds
- 1 tsp sweet paprika powder
- 1200 ml vegetable broth
- 150 g small mushrooms
- 200 g sour cream
- ½ fret fresh parsley (for garnishing)

## Preparation:

1. Put all the ingredients into your soup maker except sour cream
2. Please check your soup maker's maximum and minimum lines and adjust the fluid levels accordingly. Don't exceed the maximum limit and keep the fluid level between the minimum and maximum.
3. Set your soup maker to the "Smooth" setting.
4. Once the soup is ready, taste and season it if necessary.
5. Add the sour cream and stir it well.
6. Serve hot with Foccacia bread and chopped parsley on top.

# Chestnut Cream Soup

- Cooking time: 30 minutes
- Servings 4

## *Ingredients:*

- 1 onion (small)
- 1 tbsp oil
- 400 g chestnuts (cooked)
- 1500 ml of vegetable stock
- 200 ml double cream ((lower fat: Creme fraiche))
- A pinch of thyme
- 1 pinch of salt
- 1 pinch of pepper
- 1 pinch of nutmeg (grated)

## *Preparation:*

1. Put all the ingredients into your soup maker except double cream.
2. Please check your soup maker's maximum and minimum lines and adjust the fluid levels accordingly. Don't exceed the maximum limit and keep the fluid level between the minimum and maximum.
3. Set your soup maker to the "Smooth" setting.
4. Once the soup is ready, taste and season it if necessary.
5. Add the double cream and stir it well.
6. Serve hot.

# Cabbage Soup

- Cooking time: 30 min
- Servings 4

## *Ingredients*

- 1 small white cabbage shredded
- 3 peppers (red, yellow, green) chopped
- 2 medium onions, chopped
- 1 bunch of celery, chopped
- 1 can of chopped tomatoes (400 g )
- 1 l vegetable stock (more depending on the amount of water)
- Salt & pepper
- 1 pinch of chilli powder (optional)
- Cumin (taste)

## *Preparation:*

1. Put all the ingredients into your soup maker.
2. Please check your soup maker's maximum and minimum lines and adjust the fluid levels accordingly. Don't exceed the maximum limit and keep the fluid level between the minimum and maximum.
3. Set your soup maker to the "Chunky" setting.
4. Once the soup is ready, taste and season it if necessary.
5. Add more cumin to taste.

# White Wine Soup

- Cooking time: 25 minutes
- Servings: 2

## *Ingredients*

- 600 ml of vegetable stock
- 400 ml white wine
- 150 ml single cream
- 1 tbsp butter
- 5 egg yolks
- salt
- pepper
- nutmeg
- 1/2 bunch of chives (cut into fine rolls) for garnishing

## *Preparation:*

1. Put all the ingredients into your soup maker except chives.
2. Please check your soup maker's maximum and minimum lines and adjust the fluid levels accordingly. Don't exceed the maximum limit and keep the fluid level between the minimum and maximum.
3. Set your soup maker to the "Smooth" setting.
4. Once the soup is ready, taste and season it if necessary.
5. Serve with toasted bread, cheese platter and salami.

# Creamy Cress Soup

- Cooking time: 25 minutes
- Servings: 2

## *Ingredients:*

- 2 shallots
- 30 g butter
- 40 g flour
- 500 ml classic vegetable broth
- 4 quail eggs
- 100 ml single cream
- 120 g watercress
- salt
- pepper
- 2 tbsp walnut oil

## *Preparation:*

1. Put all the ingredients into your soup maker except yoghurt, lemon juice and garlic.
2. Please check your soup maker's maximum and minimum lines and adjust the fluid levels accordingly. Don't exceed the maximum limit and keep the fluid level between the minimum and maximum.
3. Set your soup maker to the "Smooth" setting.
4. Whilst cooking, mix yoghurt, lemon juice and crushed garlic
5. Once the soup is ready, taste and season it if necessary.
6. Add the garlicky yoghurt mixture and stir it well.
   Serve hot with warm cornbread and olives.

# Cauliflower, Carrot and Cumin Soup

- Cooking Time: 30 minutes
- Serves: 4
- Diet: Vegetarian, Vegan, low calorie

## *Ingredients:*

- 750 ml water
- 2 chicken cubes(vegetable cubes for vegan alternative)
- 1 large Cauliflower head (chopped)
- 2 medium carrots (grated)
- 2 tablespoon double cream(soy cream for vegan option)
- 1 teaspoon of cumin seeds
- Salt and pepper to taste

## *Preparation:*

1. Chop the cauliflower heads into a small size and grate some carrots.
2. Put all the ingredients in your soup maker apart from cream and cumin seeds.
3. Set your soup maker to the "Smooth" setting and cook.
4. Once cooked, season to taste.
5. Transfer it to a bowl.
6. Add some cream and stir it well
7. Serve it with a sprinkle of cumin seeds on top.

# Broccoli and Stilton Soup

- Cooking time: 25 minutes
- Servings: 2

## *Ingredients:*

- 2 tbsp vegetable oil
- 1 onion, finely chopped
- 1 stick celery, sliced
- 1 leek, sliced
- 1 medium potato, diced
- 1l chicken or vegetable stock
- 1 head of broccoli, roughly chopped
- 160g stilton, crumbled

## *Preparation:*

1. Chop the broccoli heads into a small size
2. Put all the ingredients in your soup maker except stilton.
3. Set your soup maker to the "Smooth" setting and cook.
4. Once cooked, season to taste.
5. Add some crumbled stilton and  stir it well
6. Serve it hot with your favourite bread.

# COLD SOUPS

# Cold Creamy Vegetable Soup

- Serves: 2-4
- Diet: Vegetarian

## *Ingredients:*

- 2 slices of whole-wheat toasted bread (soaked)
- 1 green chilli pepper
- 500 g cucumber
- 600ml cold vegetable stock
- 1 small bunch Rocket (Arugula)
- 2 garlic cloves (sliced)
- 2 spring onions (chopped)
- 1 yellow bell pepper
- 200 g light soft cheese
- 3 tbsp white wine vinegar
- 2 tbsp olive oil
- Salt and Pepper to taste
- Green Tabasco to taste

## *Preparation:*

1. Put all the ingredients into your soup maker.
2. Choose the "Blend" setting and blitz until it is smooth
3. Check the consistency of the soup, and add more cold stock/water if needed
4. Season with salt and pepper if necessary, and add a little Tabasco.
5. Keep the soup cold for 2 hours; it tastes best when it's very chilled!
6. Dice the cucumber and the celery stick, set aside before serving, and then sprinkle over the cold broth.

# Cold Beet Soup with Eggs

- Serves: 2-4
- Diet: Vegetarian

## *Ingredients:*

- 2 eggs (Boiled)
- 500 g beetroot (pre-cooked; vacuumed, chopped)
- 1 clove of garlic
- 750 ml vegetable broth
- 70 g Greek yoghurt
- 100 ml single cream
- 2 tbsp rapeseed oil
- ½ organic lemon (zest and juice)
- 1 pinch of chilli powder
- 1 tsp sweet paprika powder
- 1/4 teaspoon salt
- 1/8 teaspoon pepper
- 20 g young beetroot leaf (1 handful -optional)

## *Preparation:*

- Boil eggs hard in boiling water for 8-10 minutes; quench cold, let cool and peel.
- Put everything into your soup maker except eggs.
- Please check the Max and Min lines and adjust the fluid accordingly. Don't exceed the maximum limit and keep the fluid between the minimum and maximum levels.
- Set your soup maker to a "Blend/Smoothie" setting.
- Blend it until it is smooth and chill for 30 min-1 hr
- Season to taste and serve chilled.

# Tomato Gazpacho with Celery

- Preparation: 10 min
- Servings: 4
- Diet: Vegetarian, Vegan, Low Calorie

## *Ingredients:*

- 450 g cherry tomatoes
- 2 spring onions
- 1 bell pepper
- 250 g cucumber (half cucumber)
- 2 cloves of garlic
- 2 red chilli pepper or jalapeno
- 20 g basil (a bunch)
- 400 ml strained tomatoes (Passata)
- 500 ml ice-cold water
- 2 tbsp sherry vinegar
- ¼ teaspoon salt
- ¼ teaspoon pepper
- 150 g celery (2 sticks- save one for garnishing)
- 2 tbsp olive oil
- 1 tbsp white wine vinegar

## *Preparation:*

- Put everything into your soup maker. You may add some ice-cold water to make it smoother.
- Please check the Max and Min lines and adjust the fluid accordingly. Don't exceed the maximum limit and keep the fluid between the minimum and maximum levels.
- Set your soup maker to a "Blend" setting and blend until it is smooth.
- Season to taste.
- Chill in the fridge for 30 minutes to 1 hr before serving
- Serve with a celery stick
- You may even turn this beautiful summery soup into a "Bloody Mary" by adding some vodka and maybe more Tabasco and Worcestershire sauce splashes.

# No-Fuss Strawberry Gazpacho

- Preparation: 15 minutes, Chilling :30 min -1 hr
- Servings: 4
- Diet: Vegetarian

## *Ingredients:*

- 500 g strawberries
- ½ small watermelon
- 1 red bell pepper
- 1 small chilli pepper
- 2 spring onions
- 10 g mint (0.5 bunch)
- 2 tbsp lemon juice
- 200 ml tomato juice
- 250 ml cold water
- Salt & pepper to taste

## *Preparation:*

- Put everything into your soup maker. You may add some more ice-cold water to make it smoother.
- Please check the Max and Min lines and adjust the fluid accordingly. Don't exceed the maximum limit and keep the fluid between the minimum and maximum levels.
- Set your soup maker to a "Blend" setting and blend until it is smooth.
- Season to taste.
- Chill in the fridge for 30 minutes to 1 hr before serving.

# Bread Soup with Dried Fruit and Whipped Cream

- Cooking time: 30 min
- Serves: 2-4
- Diet: Dessert, Vegetarian

## *Ingredients:*

- 500 g rye bread
- 1.5 l water
- 150 g dried fruits (raisins, cranberries, apples, plums, apricots, any of your choice)
- 150 brown sugars
- 2 tablespoons lemon juice
- Pinch of cinnamon
- Whipped cream or vanilla ice cream (for garnishing)

## *Preparation:*

1. Toast the rye bread for 4 minutes on your toaster or grill until they are brown.
2. Add all the ingredients to the soup maker except dried fruits and whipped cream
3. Choose the "Smooth" setting and cook.
4. Once cooked, add the dried fruits and give the soup a good stir.
5. Chill in the fridge for an hour before serving,
6. Serve with whipped cream or a dollop of vanilla ice cream.

# Cold Avocado and Cucumber Soup

- Cooking Time: 15 minutes
- Serves: 4

## *Ingredients:*

- 2 ripe avocadoes (peeled, stones removed)
- 1-2 large cucumbers (appx. 400 gr. peeled, cut)
- 4 spring onions (chopped)
- 2 limes juice
- 300 g plain yoghurt (low fat or total fat)
- 750 ml classic vegetable broth
- Salt & black pepper to taste
- 3 tbsp vegetarian caviar or lumpfish roe (optional- to garnish)
- 1 bunch of chives (to garnish)

## *Preparation:*

1. Put everything into your soup maker except vegetarian caviar/lumpfish roe and chives.
2. Please check the Max and Min lines and adjust the fluid accordingly. Don't exceed the maximum limit and keep the fluid between the minimum and maximum levels.
3. Set your soup maker to a "Blend" setting and blend until it is smooth.
4. Chill for at least 1 hour.
5. Wash the chives, shake dry and cut into fine rolls.
6. Pour the soup into chilled cups or glasses and place 1 tablespoon of caviar/lumpfish roe on each bowl.
7. Serve sprinkled with chives.

# Cold Watermelon Soup

- Preparation: 15 minutes
- Serves: 4-6
- Diet: Vegetarian, Vegan

## Ingredients:

- 1 lemon (zest and juice)
- 1 kg small watermelon (0.5 small watermelons) (chopped)
- 400 g peeled fresh tomatoes (Substitutes A can of chopped/plum tomatoes or passata)
- 100 ml water
- Salt and black pepper to taste
- 1 stem basil (to garnish)
- 1 tbsp yoghurt – Vegan yoghurt option (to garnish)

## Preparation:

1. Put all the ingredients into your soup maker.
2. Please check the Max and Min lines and adjust the fluid accordingly. Don't exceed the maximum limit and keep the fluid between the minimum and maximum levels.
3. Set your soup maker to a "Blend" setting and blend for 10 seconds intervals until it is smooth.
4. Serve the soup with basil leaves and 1 tablespoon of yoghurt on top.

# Chilled Tomato and Sweet Melon soup

- Cooking time: 30 min
- Serves: 2-4

## *Ingredients:*

- 5-6 fresh medium size tomatoes (cut into chunky cubes)
- 1-2 medium-size cantaloupe melons (peeled, cut into chunky cubes)
- 1 small chilli pepper (chopped)
- 2 small bell pepper (chopped-deseeded)
- 2 limes juice and 1 lime zest
- 500 ml tomato juice
- 200 ml water
- Salt& Pepper to taste
- 2 spring onions (to garnish)
- 4 stems of mint (to garnish)
- 4 tsp olive oil (to garnish)

## *Preparation:*

1. Put all the ingredients into your soup maker except spring onions, mint and olive oil.
2. Please check the Max and Min lines and adjust the fluid accordingly. Don't exceed the maximum limit and keep the fluid between the minimum and maximum levels.
3. Choose the "Blend" setting and blend the ingredients until they are smooth.
4. Check the soup's consistency and add more water If necessary.
5. Season to taste
6. Serve, sprinkle with spring onions and mint, and drizzle with 1 teaspoon of oil.

# Chilled Lemony Sweet Melon Soup

- Cooking time: 15 minutes
- Serves: 2-4
- Diet: Vegetarian, Vegan

## *Ingredients*

- 750 g watermelon ( peeled, cut; well chilled)
- 7 branches of lemon thyme (stripped)
- 200 ml classic vegetable broth
- A pinch of salt and  cracked black pepper to taste
- 200 ml apple juice
- 1 tablespoon honey

## *Preparation:*

1. Put all the ingredients into your soup maker.
2. Please check the Max and Min lines and adjust the fluid accordingly. Don't exceed the maximum limit and keep the fluid between the minimum and maximum levels.
3. Set your soup maker to a "Blend" setting. Blend the mixture until it is smooth.
4. Season to taste if necessary.
5. Chill it in the fridge overnight or at least one hour before serving.

# Cold Cucumber Soup

- Cooking time: 30 minutes
- Serves: 2- 4
- Diet: Vegetarian

## *Ingredients:*

- 3 large cucumbers
- 4-6 garlic (crushed)
- 4 tablespoons of rice wine vinegar or white wine vinegar
- A bunch of dills (chopped)
- 650 ml beef stock (cold)
- 100 ml light single cream
- 500 g light yoghurt
- Salt & Pepper
- 1 tbsp olive oil

## *Preparation:*

1. Wash the cucumber and cut it into large pieces. Marinate with salt, crushed garlic and balsamic vinegar for a few minutes.
2. Add the dill, cold beef soup and yoghurt and put other ingredients into your soup maker.
3. Choose the "Blend" option and blend until it is smooth.
4. Season to taste with salt and pepper.
5. Fill deep chilled plates and drizzle olive oil over them if necessary.

# Cold Avocado and Cucumber Soup

- Chilling Time: 30 min
- Servings 2
- Diet: Vegetarian

## *Ingredients:*

- 200 g avocado (1 avocado)
- 125 g mini cucumber (1 mini cucumber)
- 2 spring onions
- 1 lime
- 150 g yoghurt (0.3% fat)
- 300 ml classic vegetable broth
- salt
- pepper
- 2 tbsp vegetarian caviar
- 1 bunch chives

## *Preparation::*

1. Halve the avocado and remove the stone
2. Then remove the pulp from the skin.
3. Peel the cucumber and cut it in half lengthways.
4. Scrape out the seeds with a spoon.
5. Wash and clean the spring onions. Roughly chop the onions, cucumber, and avocado.
6. Squeeze the lime.
7. Finely puree the onion, cucumber and avocado pieces with yoghurt, vegetable stock, 2 tbsp lime juice, salt, and pepper in your soup maker.
8. Chill for at least 30 min. Wash the chives, shake dry and cut into fine rolls.
9. Pour the soup into chilled cups or glasses and place 1 tablespoon of caviar on top.
10. Serve them sprinkled with chives.

# All About Erde:

Erde has been a freelance writer for Eve publishing for some time. He is the mastermind behind the idea of creating soup maker recipes for any practical, sometimes downright lazy person like himself. He is a foodie and a soup junkie, a globe-trotter. He gathers soup recipes from his travels to Europe and the Middle East. Travelling around the globe and seeing different cultures and countries is one of his passions. He lives in the UK, where cold and rainy days are a blessing for his soup recipes.

## If you are enjoying this product, please leave us a review on Amazon:

### How to leave us a review?
5- Go to your Amazon Account
6- Click "Your Orders"
7- Find and click this product
8- Click on "Write a product review."

## Your opinion matters to us!!!
We are happy to take your words on board and listen to your ideas. This is so important for us to develop more product ideas according to your needs in the future.

If you enjoy this product and/or have any suggestions. Please contact us at contact@evepublishing.co.uk

# © Copyright 2022 - All rights reserved.

The content contained within this book may not be reproduced, duplicated, or transmitted without direct written permission from the author or the publisher.
Under no circumstances will any blame or legal responsibility be held against the publisher, or author, for any damages, reparation, or monetary loss due to the information contained within this book. Either directly or indirectly.

Legal Notice:
This book is copyright protected. This book is only for personal use. You cannot amend, distribute, sell, use, quote, or paraphrase any part of the content within this book without the author or publisher's consent.

Disclaimer Notice:
Please note the information contained within this document is for educational and entertainment purposes only. All effort has been executed to present accurate, up-to-date, and reliable, complete information. No warranties of any kind are declared or implied. Readers acknowledge that the author is not engaging in the rendering of legal, financial, medical, or professional advice. The content within this book has been derived from various sources. Please consult a licensed professional before attempting any techniques outlined in this book. By reading this document, the reader agrees that under no circumstances is the author responsible for any losses, direct or indirect, which are incurred as a result of the use of the information contained within this document, including, but not limited to, — errors, omissions, or inaccuracies.

Printed in Great Britain
by Amazon

57904910R00075